MICHAEL POLANYI

LIBRARY OF MODERN THINKERS

PUBLISHER: T. KENNETH CRIBB JR.
SERIES EDITOR: JEREMY BEER

PUBLISHED TITLES

ROBERT NISBET *by Brad Lowell Stone*

LUDWIG VON MISES *by Israel M. Kirzner*

WILHELM RÖPKE *by John Zmirak*

ERIC VOEGELIN *by Michael P. Federici*

BERTRAND DE JOUVENEL *by Daniel J. Mahoney*

MICHAEL POLANYI *by Mark T. Mitchell*

FORTHCOMING

CHRISTOPHER DAWSON *by Gerald Russello*

WILL HERBERG *by Vigen Guroian*

WILLMOORE KENDALL *by George Carey*

CHRISTOPHER LASCH *by Alan Woolfolk*

ANDREW NELSON LYTLE *by Mark Malvasi*

JOHN COURTNEY MURRAY *by Marc Guerra*

MICHAEL OAKESHOTT *by Timothy Fuller*

RICHARD WEAVER *by Steven Ealy*

FRANCIS GRAHAM WILSON *by H. Lee Cheek*

MICHAEL POLANYI

THE ART OF KNOWING

Mark T. Mitchell

PATRICK HENRY COLLEGE

ISI BOOKS
WILMINGTON, DELAWARE
2006

The Library of Modern Thinkers is published in cooperation with Collegiate Network, Inc. Generous grants from the Sarah Scaife Foundation, Earhart Foundation, F. M. Kirby Foundation, Castle Rock Foundation, Pierre F. and Enid Goodrich Foundation, Wilbur Foundation, and the William H. Donner Foundation made this series possible. The Intercollegiate Studies Institute and Collegiate Network, Inc., gratefully acknowledge their support.

Mitchell, Mark T.

Michael Polanyi : the art of knowing / Mark T. Mitchell. — 1st ed. — Wilmington, Del. : ISI Books, c2006.

p. ; cm.
(Library of modern thinkers)

ISBN-13: 978-1-932236-90-3; 978-1-932236-91-0
ISBN-10: 1-932236-90-2 (cloth); 1-932236-91-0 (pbk.)
Includes bibliographical references and index.

1. Polanyi, Michael, 1891– 2. Polanyi, Michael, 1891–, Criticism and interpretation. 3. Philosophers—Biography. 4. Social scientists—Biography. 5. Philosophy, Modern. 6. Social science. I. Title.

b945.p584 m58 2006
192—dc22   0607

Library of Congress Control Number: 2006921347

Published in the United States by:
ISI Books
In cooperation with Collegiate Network, Inc.
Post Office Box 4431
Wilmington, DE 19807-0431

Cover and interior design by Sam Torode

Manufactured in the United States of America

CONTENTS

Acknowledgments

No BOOK IS THE PRODUCT of a solitary individual. Whether the author admits it or not, many contribute, in various ways, to its creation. Unfortunately, it is impossible to trace completely the lines of influence, the manifold ways that different people add to the content or alter the direction of the investigation. Fully aware of these limitations, I am happy to recognize some of those who helped to make this book what it is.

First, I would like to thank George W. Carey of Georgetown University. I could not have asked for a more wise and gracious mentor. Since our graduate student years at Georgetown, Richard Avramenko has been a good friend. Our long conversations over Homeric meals have been a source of great enjoyment as well as intellectual stimulation.

The administration of Patrick Henry College has encouraged my writing and helped me to carve out time from a busy schedule to pursue this and other projects. Additionally, I am grateful for the students I am privileged to teach, especially those in the political theory program. Their enthusiasm for learning makes teaching a joy.

Walter Mead read and commented on the entire manuscript. His deep understanding of Polanyi's thought proved invaluable. Furthermore, an anonymous reader provided good advice and helpful suggestions. I am thankful also to Jeff Nelson of ISI Books for seeing the merits of this project and giving me the opportunity to pursue it. Jeremy Beer of ISI Books has been a source of constant encouragement and sound advice. His passion for ideas and his editorial expertise have made this a much better book. Thank you also to ISI's Jennifer Connolly. Her cheerful, prompt, and expert assistance was indispensable.

Parts of chapter five first appeared in articles published in the *Journal of Religious Ethics* as "Personal Participation: Michael Polanyi, Eric Voegelin, and the Indispensability of Faith" and in *Tradition & Discovery: The Polanyi Society Periodical* as "Michael Polanyi and Michael Oakeshott: Common Ground, Uncommon Foundations." I am grateful to Blackwell Publishing and *Tradition & Discovery* for permission to reprint this material.

Finally, closer to home, my three sons, Seth, Noah, and Scott are the young men who make my life full. Their laughter, trust, and love inspire me every day. My wife, Joby, has my eternal gratitude and devotion. This book is dedicated to her.

Preface

THE TWENTIETH CENTURY was a time of marked contrasts. On the one hand, there were significant advances in standards of living (at least in the West); technological wonders brought the world together, as space was annihilated by electronic communication and air travel; lives were extended and health improved with the advent of penicillin, vaccinations, and organ transplants. But there was a dark side. With increased material wealth came a fixation on material goods and gain; increased mobility led to the fragmentation of families and communities; technological advances brought the potential to kill on a scale previously only dreamed of by madmen and prophets; advances in medicine have brought us to the age of biotechnology, where the very nature of the human species seems nearly within our manipulative grasp. Yeats, writing in 1920, surveyed the wreckage of Europe and penned words that described the scene and predicted with clear-sighted vision the moral and political chaos yet to be unleashed:

Things fall apart; the center cannot hold;
Mere anarchy is loosed upon the world,
The blood-dimmed tide is loosed, and everywhere
The ceremony of innocence is drowned;
The best lack all conviction, while the worst
Are full of passionate intensity.[1]

The twentieth century witnessed both stunning advances in science and technology as well as the bloodiest killing spree in history. The convergence of these two facts is, in retrospect, not surprising. Optimism—optimism born of success—was clearly warranted in the realm of the sciences. But there were not corresponding advances in our moral understanding. Rather, a kind of skepticism came to maturity. Skepticism had, of course, long been in view—at first just on the horizon, no bigger than a man's hand, but steadily growing until it blotted the Western sky. Our wild advances in knowledge, it seems, did not automatically translate into advances in wisdom. As T. S. Eliot wrote:

Endless invention, endless experiment,
Brings knowledge of motion, but not of stillness;
Knowledge of speech, but not of silence;
Knowledge of words, and ignorance of the Word.
All our knowledge brings us nearer to our ignorance,
All our ignorance brings us nearer to death,
But nearness to death no nearer to GOD.
Where is the Life we have lost in living?
Where is the wisdom we have lost in knowledge?
Where is the knowledge we have lost in information?

The cycles of Heaven in twenty centuries
Bring us farther from GOD and nearer to the Dust.[2]

The advances of modern science, marked by so many obvious successes, gave science and the methods of scientific investigation a pride of place. But this also created a sense of autonomy that, when coupled with advancing moral and religious skepticism, served to make scientific and technological progress appear inevitable and moral and spiritual checks on that progress unnecessary. In this climate, the stage was set for utopian aspirations to run their course unhindered by the very forces that in an earlier age would have moderated them—and perhaps even strangled them in their infancy. Indeed, one might well describe the twentieth century as the bloodiest period of utopian political experimentation the world has ever witnessed.

Born in Budapest in 1891, Michael Polanyi came of age when the optimism of the early years of the new century was eclipsed by the horrors of the Great War. His firsthand encounter with modern warfare and later with totalitarianism in the form of both fascism and communism convinced this world-class physical chemist that the very foundations of civilization were in jeopardy. Polanyi recognized that the prevailing conception of the scientific enterprise—characterized by the ideal of the disinterested scientist's strict detachment from his subject matter, which could ultimately be reduced to physics and chemistry—was seriously inadequate and ultimately misleading. The scientist, according to Polanyi, is no dispassionate observer; instead, he is passionate in his quest to make contact with a reality that he necessarily believes is real and knowable. Furthermore, the practice of science requires an antecedent commitment on the part of its practitioners to such transcendent values as truth, justice, and charity. Finally, these values must exist in the context of a community of scientists who pass on the values of science to aspiring young scientists, as a master trains an apprentice. Thus, according to Polanyi, science depends for its success on such things as tradition, submission to authority, personal commitment, and moral ideals.

Polanyi's career as a scientist was characterized by creative brilliance; there were those who believed he would eventually win a Nobel Prize in chemistry. But as the war-to-end-all-wars turned out merely to prepare the way for even worse political disorder, Polanyi's concerns turned gradually toward the problem of defending a free society against tyranny in all its forms. He first focused on economics and the practice of science. He was convinced that the success of both required liberty, and that "planned" science would destroy science, just as a "planned" economy would result in hunger and privation. But as he continued to consider the necessary foundations of a free society, Polanyi became convinced that at root the political terror of the twentieth century was the result of a conception of knowledge that refused to admit that moral and spiritual concepts have any real existence. Bereft of these, individual and political action is limited merely by imagination and will. To counter this descent into the moral abyss, Polanyi argued that a new conception of knowledge must be introduced—a conception that once again acknowledged the reality of moral and spiritual ideals to which free and responsible men and women can commit themselves in service to a truth rooted in reality which is infinitely richer than that assumed by reductionistic mate-

rialism. Thus, although Polanyi's nonscientific work spans a wide
range of disciplines, including philosophy of science, economics,
theology, and epistemology, all of these pursuits spring from a
common concern: a tireless attempt to reestablish a legitimate
grounding for liberty. In this light, Polanyi should be understood
as a political philosopher who rightly grasped that liberty depends
on resources beyond politics.

ABBREVIATIONS

All page references in the text are to Polanyi's writings. When referring to his books and articles, I use the following abbreviations:

BOOKS

CF   *Contempt of Freedom: The Russian Experiment and After* (New York: Arno Press, 1975).

FEFT   *Full Employment and Free Trade* (London: Cambridge University Press, 1945).

KB   *Knowing and Being*, ed. Marjorie Grene (London: Routledge & Kegan Paul, 1969).

LL   *Logic of Liberty* (Indianapolis: Liberty Fund, 1998).

M   *Meaning*, with Harry Prosch (Chicago: University of Chicago Press, 1975).

PK   *Personal Knowledge: Toward a Post-Critical Philosophy* (Chicago: University of Chicago Press, 1958).

SEP   *Society, Economics, and Philosophy: Selected Papers*, ed. R. T. Allen (New Brunswick, NJ: Transaction Publishers, 1997).

SFS   *Science, Faith, and Society* (Chicago: University of Chicago Press, 1964).

SM   *The Study of Man* (Chicago: University of Chicago Press, 1958).

STSR *Scientific Thought and Social Reality: Essays by Michael Polanyi*, ed. Fred Schwartz (New York: International Universities Press, 1973).

TD   *The Tacit Dimension* (Garden City, NY: Doubleday & Company, 1966).

ARTICLES

CI   "Creative Imagination," *Tri-Quarterly* (Fall 1966): 111–23. Also published in *Chemical and Engineering News* 44 (1966): 85–93.

FR   "Faith and Reason," *Journal of Religion* 41, no. 4 (1961): 237–47.

LP   "Logic and Psychology," *American Psychologist* 23 (1968): 27–43.

OMM   "On the Modern Mind," *Encounter* 24 (May 1965): 12–20.

SB   "The Stability of Beliefs," *British Journal for the Philosophy of Science* 3, no. 11 (1952): 217–32.

SR   "Science and Religion," *Philosophy Today* 7 (1963): 4–14.

CHAPTER ONE

LIFE AND TIMES OF MICHAEL POLANYI

BY HIS OWN ADMISSION, Michael Polanyi turned to philosophy as an afterthought to his successful career as a scientist. This transition was officially recognized in 1948, when a Chair of Social Studies was created for him at the University of Manchester, where he had served as head of Physical Chemistry since 1933. With over two hundred scientific publications to his name, he was a prominent figure whose research focused mainly on three areas: adsorption of gases on solids, x-ray structure analysis of the properties of solids, and the rate of chemical reactions. Polanyi was unusual even as a scientist in that he was active in both theoretical and experimental work. A keen mind coupled with a rigorous and broad liberal education provided him with the capacity to pursue interests outside of his field of expertise; the political upheavals of twentieth-century Europe provided the catalyst.

Polanyi was born in Budapest in 1891—the fifth child in an extraordinary family. Michael's father, born Mihaly Pollacsek, was a successful railroad financier. While living in Vienna, he met and later married Cecile Wohl, the daughter of Andreas Wohl, a scholar of some distinction from what is today Vilnius, Lithuania. Both Mihaly and Cecile were of Jewish families, generally liberal, and nonreligious. In Vienna, Cecile gave birth to their first four children. One year prior to Michael's birth, the family moved to Budapest, magyarized the family name, and entered the elite circle of Hungarian intellectuals.

Both Mihaly and Cecile-Mama, as she was called, were intellectually serious and sought to provide the best education possible for their children. Private tutors were hired to teach the children English and French in addition to the German and Hungarian spoken at home. The children's education was regimented and Spartan: "In the morning a cold shower, an hour of gymnastics, hot cocoa with a roll, Schiller and Goethe, Corneille and Racine."[1] The intellectual climate in Budapest at the time was vibrant, and Cecile-Mama established a salon that attracted a wide variety of artists and writers. As Polanyi later described it, "I grew up in this circle, dreaming of great things."[2]

In 1900 this pleasant existence changed dramatically. Months of steady rain washed out the rail line Mihaly had been building. He went bankrupt, and the family was forced to move to humbler quarters while he took work as a consultant. In 1905, when Michael was fourteen, Mihaly died. By that time, Michael was attending the Minta Gymnasium, a top-notch humanistic school, but the family's new financial situation required him to tutor the sons of wealthy families to help make ends meet. During his eight years at the Minta Gymnasium, he studied history, literature, language, science, and mathematics. By his own admission, physics and art history were his favorite subjects—an early foreshadowing of the breadth of interest that would characterize the rest of his life.

Polanyi's education continued at the University of Budapest, where he enrolled in the medical program. In 1910, at the age of nineteen, he published his first academic paper: "Contribution to the Chemistry of the Hydrocephalic Liquid." From then on, Polanyi published papers every year (excluding 1912) for over six decades—first in science, then in economics, politics, and the philosophy of science as his attention gradually shifted to these areas during the 1930s and '40s. His last scientific paper was published in 1949.

While at the University of Budapest, he became involved with the Galileo Circle, a student organization committed to a scientific understanding of social, economic, and political issues. Michael's older brother Karl was the group's first president. Michael himself was an active member in the circle's "Committee on Natural Science" and occasionally gave talks on physics and chemistry. Paul Ignotus, also a member of the circle, later noted Polanyi's "liberality of mind, the simultaneity of personal and technical interests, and the ability to coordinate them in behavior as well as in philosophy." In addition to a mind capable of synthesizing disparate concepts, Ignotus noted that Polanyi possessed a unique character trait: "What made him differ most from those around him was his reverence."[3] This reverence extended both to the subject matter at hand as well as to the people with whom he dealt. Polanyi's love of discovery propelled him to extend his inquiries into a wide variety of avenues, and people with whom he associated found him congenial and polite.

Michael Polanyi's interest in pure science, especially chemistry, was always stronger than his interest in medicine. In 1913–14, he spent a year in Karlsruhe, Germany, studying physical chemistry. During that time, he focused on thermodynamics. After Polanyi wrote a paper describing his findings, his mentor, Professor Georg Bredig, sent it off to Albert Einstein—the most competent person to judge Polanyi's findings. Einstein was impressed: "The papers of your M. Polanyi please me a lot. I have checked over the essentials in them and found them fundamentally correct." As Polanyi later described it, "Bang! I was created a scientist."[4] Polanyi exchanged several letters with Einstein at that time and their correspondence, though irregular, continued for twenty years. Such attention provided powerful encouragement to the young Polanyi. And it further convinced him that his true calling was in fact chemistry, not medicine.

Shortly after Michael returned to Budapest in the summer of 1914, the World War began. Although his medical training had not included the internship that would have qualified him to practice, field doctors were needed. He volunteered for service and became a military physician assigned to a field hospital. He soon contracted diphtheria and was forced to spend several months convalescing. He returned to his duties only to become ill again, and for the remainder of the war he was given light duty. During his time in military hospitals, he managed to write and revise several scientific papers. One, "Adsorption of Gases by a Solid Non-Volatile Absorbent," was published in the *Proceedings of the German Physical Society* in 1916. Polanyi then translated the paper into Hungarian and submitted it as a PhD dissertation to Dr. Gustav

Buchböck, a chemist at the University of Budapest. Years later, Polanyi would describe an exchange that anticipated a central insight in his understanding of the process of discovery:

> The Professor of mathematical physics, to whom my paper was assigned [to verify the mathematics], had never heard of my subject matter. He studied my work bit by bit and then asked me to explain a curious point; my result seemed correct, but its derivation faulty. Admitting my mistake I said that surely one first draws one's conclusions and then puts their derivations right. The professor just stared at me.[5]

Polanyi had already secured a teaching position at the University of Budapest when he was officially awarded his degree—an unusual process, to be sure. His academic training had been no more orthodox. Formally trained in medicine, he had practiced only under the duress of war. And his degree in chemistry had been granted on the basis of a paper that had already been published. His later essays in economics, philosophy of science, political theory, and epistemology were all written from the vantage point of an outsider. This is doubtless one reason why Polanyi's nonscientific work has not received the attention it deserves. This is not to say that professionals in these various fields jealously protected their turf from an upstart outsider (though this might at times have been the case); rather, because he was an outsider, his methods and vocabulary were often unconventional. He did not always situate himself within current debates or the history of the particular discipline he was addressing. As a result, it was difficult for more conventional practitioners to categorize his thought or respond to it adequately.

Polanyi recognized this apparent defect in his education as an asset. He was, in a sense, immune to the commitments and distractions of his contemporaries, who generally approached their subjects in more traditional fashion. This was true of his work in chemistry and doubly true for his later work in philosophy. As Polanyi describes it,

> I believe that I came into my true vocation in 1946 when I set out on the pursuit of a new philosophy to meet the need of our age. My way at starting with little or no schooling was wholly beneficial here. For a sound knowledge of philosophy makes the necessary radical advances extremely difficult; one must shoot here first and ask questions afterwards, as I have always done—for better or worse.[6]

There was a downside to his unconventional education. In 1921, for example, Polanyi was invited by Fritz Haber, a Nobel Laureate chemist, to present his theory of adsorption to the Kaiser Wilhelm Institute for Physical Chemistry. Einstein was specially invited to attend. Both Einstein and Haber severely attacked the theory, accusing Polanyi of displaying "a total disregard for the scientifically established structure of matter." As Polanyi put it later, "professionally, I survived by the skin of my teeth" (KB, 89). However, he still believed his theory was correct. A decade later, physicist Fritz London's groundbreaking work on cohesive forces suggested a breakthrough. Polanyi contacted him, London carried out the necessary computations, and in 1930 they jointly published a paper vindicating Polanyi's theory of adsorption. Although some years were required for it to be accepted, the theory is now recognized as an integral part of the discipline. In a 1963 essay, Polanyi reflected on the lessons he had learned from this experience:

> I would never have conceived my theory, let alone have made a great effort to verify it, if I had been more familiar with major developments in physics that were taking place. Moreover, my initial ignorance of the powerful false objections that were raised against my ideas protected those ideas from being nipped in the bud. Later, by undertaking the labor necessary to verify my theory, I became immune to these objections, but I remained powerless to refute them. My verification could make no impression on minds convinced that it was bound to be specious (KB, 91).

Yet even though Polanyi was right and some of the greatest minds of the time turned out to be mistaken, he did not believe that his critics had deviated from proper scientific procedure:

> Could this miscarriage of the scientific method have been avoided? I do not think so. There must be at all times a predominantly accepted scientific view of the nature of things, in the light of which research is jointly conducted by members of the community of scientists. A strong presumption that any evidence which contradicts this view is invalid must prevail. Such evidence has to be disregarded, even if it cannot be accounted for, in the hope that it will eventually turn out to be false or irrelevant. . . . Discipline *must* remain severe and is in fact severe (KB, 92, 93).

The idea that discipline is a necessary component for the development and success of science is often ignored or even denied. Polanyi

quotes Bertrand Russell, who argues—naïvely, in Polanyi's view—
that science obviates the need for authority. According to Russell,

> the triumphs of science are due to the substitution of observation
> and inference for authority. Every attempt to revive authority in
> intellectual matters is a retrograde step. And it is part of the scien-
> tific attitude that the pronouncements of science do not claim to
> be certain, but only the most probable on the basis of present
> evidence. One of the great benefits that science confers upon those
> who understand its spirit is that it enables them to live without
> the delusive support of subjective authority (KB, 94).

In Polanyi's view, Russell could not be more wrong. "Such state-
ments obscure the fact that the authority of current scientific
opinion is indispensable to the discipline of scientific institutions;
that its functions are invaluable, even though its dangers are an
unceasing menace to scientific progress" (KB, 94).

During the war, Polanyi's interests began to expand. His first
political writing was published in 1917, as the war still raged. Polanyi
later described the piece titled "To the Peacemakers: Views on the
Prerequisites of War and Peace in Europe" as "an attack on the
materialist conception of history."[7] He argued that a lasting peace
could not be forged unless ancient hatreds and prejudices were
first removed. If that could occur, Polanyi saw the possibility of a
united and prosperous Europe—a Europe that could build on the
freedom of movement and intellectual vibrancy enjoyed in the pre-
war years: "We must love a united Europe, the re-creation of our
truncated life. People leading the world should release themselves
from mutual fear and from dams built against each other. They

should seek to exploit the forces of nature and the riches of the earth, and henceforth, a new age of riches and welfare, never seen before, will open up before us" (SEP, 24). But this could not happen as long as individual states were capable of threatening each other. Polanyi argued that the state must be transcended.

> Since, as long as States can, however little, feel threatened by each other, no agreement will hinder them from taking preventative measures, and war will then break out within the shortest time from the increase of preventative measures. . . . Thus, as long as the State itself remains the supreme executive within the State, no agreement can prevent the State from developing itself to the fullest extent. . . . There is only one solution: to place the supreme power above the nations, to set up a permanent European army which would guarantee, along with the United States, the rule of our civilisation on the earth (SEP, 27).

Of special interest in this otherwise somewhat naïve piece are two sentences that presage the theory of tacit knowledge that Polanyi fully developed decades later: "Despite the fact that our age has denied 'all prejudices,' it has not freed itself from prejudices at all. For they are rooted in tacit presuppositions which determine our thoughts without our being aware of them" (SEP, 22).

An essay titled "New Skepticism" was published in 1919 in the Galileo Circle's journal *Szabadgondola*. Sounding a very different note here than in his first foray into political writing, Polanyi expresses his skepticism about the aspirations of politics. Speaking on behalf of scientists and artists, who Polanyi believes had been too easily co-opted by the political forces of the day, he argues that "[o]n account of the devastations brought by wars and revolutions we need to awake to the fact that popular belief in politics disintegrates our societies and sweeps everything away" (SEP, 29-30). Anticipating his later argument that economic and social factors are too complex to make the planning of economic systems possible, Polanyi notes that "society is so complicated that even science cannot calculate the future effects either of any institution or of any measure, and people involved in politics, with their rough minds and passionate fancies, are a thousand times less able to foresee whether the institutions they demand will meet their interests in the last analysis" (SEP, 30). Given this incapacity to calculate future effects, Polanyi argues for a new skepticism, one that mistrusts the claims of politicians and is not taken in by the irrational fears and hopes peddled by political leaders. In the wake of the devastation of the Great War, Polanyi saw an acute need for serious and rational people to reflect upon the causes of political excesses. "Our job is exploring the truth; dissecting the confused images of politics and analyzing the belief in political concepts; finding the originating conditions of political illusions and what animates the imagination to fix illusions to certain objects" (SEP, 31). Only after the underlying causes are identified and treated can politics achieve more than the mere legitimation of the abuse of power. Much of Polanyi's later work, coming during and after a second great war, was dedicated to this very project.

In the same year that "New Skepticism" was published (1919), Polanyi was baptized into the Roman Catholic Church. Dostoyevsky's Grand Inquisitor and Tolstoy's confessions of faith had led Polanyi toward Christianity.[8] Given the political wreckage that was the Europe of 1919 and the wariness of politics expressed in the "New Skepticism" piece, it is perhaps not surprising that the young Polanyi was drawn toward an institution that could provide the resources for comprehending the moral and spiritual vacuum of Europe.

After the war, conditions in Hungary gradually deteriorated. A new regime under Hungarian-born Admiral Horthy eventually took power and enacted anti-Semitic laws. As a result, Polanyi lost his job at the University of Budapest. In December 1919, he again left Hungary for Karlsruhe, Germany, where he continued his study of physical chemistry. Among the community of Hungarian students in Karlsruhe was Magda Kemeny. She was pursuing a degree in chemistry, a relatively rare thing for a woman in that day. As Magda later told him, she had once caught sight of him in Budapest dressed in his military uniform and had found him "devastatingly handsome."[9] At a Christmas party for his Hungarian friends, Polanyi designated her place with a single lily of the valley in a wine glass.

Michael and Magda were married in Budapest on February 22, 1921. They made their home in Berlin, where Polanyi had taken a position at the Institute of Fiber Chemistry in 1920. The Polanyis had two sons. George was born in 1922 and became an economist. John, born in 1929, followed in his father's footsteps. In 1986, he was awarded a Nobel Prize for his work in chemistry.

Although Polanyi was primarily interested in reaction kinetics, Fritz Haber, director of the Institute of Physical Chemistry, informed him that "reaction velocity . . . is a world problem. You should cook a piece of meat" (KB, 98). In other words, Haber admonished the eager young scientist to prove himself on a question of more manageable proportions. Polanyi complied. "Within two weeks after Polanyi joined the Fiber Institute," writes William Taussig Scott, Polanyi had "found the explanation to a peculiarly puzzling x-ray photograph of cellulose fibers, an answer that was not only far from routine but that represented the discovery of a whole new mode of x-ray analysis. In recognition of his accomplishment, Polanyi was provided with equipment and resources for a team of assistants to help him tackle problems of the structure and strength of crystal fibers."[10]

Polanyi spent his first three years in Berlin working on x-rays and crystals before migrating to Haber's Institute of Physical Chemistry. Haber was clearly satisfied that Polanyi had indeed "cooked a piece of meat." As Polanyi put it, "Haber received me now with full confidence in my ability to work as a scientist, and I immediately plunged back into reaction kinetics" (KB, 104).

During his thirteen years in Berlin, Polanyi participated in the weekly Physics Colloquium at the University of Berlin. The best and brightest physicists in the world were centered in Berlin during the 1920s, and Polanyi flourished in this intellectual climate. As he later described it, "the seminar . . . where Planck, Einstein, Schrödinger, von Laue, Hahn and Lise Meitner met every Wednesday for informal discussion is still the most glorious intellectual memory of my life."[11]

By the early 1930s, however, Germany was clearly changing. Anti-Semitism was on the rise and in academic institutions high-profile Jews were being replaced. Just prior to the Nazi takeover in 1932, Polanyi was offered the Chair of Physical Chemistry at the

University of Manchester in England. At first he hesitated. As he put it to Professor Arthur Lapworth of the University of Manchester, he was reluctant to leave Germany, "where I am rooted with the greater part of my being."[12] Polanyi was optimistic that his wartime service would insulate him from the purges then beginning. In January 1933, Polanyi finally decided to reject the offer. But just a few weeks later, he realized the gravity of his mistake. He contacted the university, accepted their offer, and the Polanyi family moved to Manchester in September of that year.

While still in Germany, Polanyi had traveled to the USSR for academic conferences in 1928, 1931, and 1932. In 1935, two years after moving to Manchester, he returned to the Soviet Union. This time he met with Nikolai Bukharin, then a leading theoretician of the Communist Party. Polanyi later recalled his conversation with him, specifically Bukharin's insistence that the

> distinction between pure and applied science made in capitalist countries was due only to the inner conflict of a type of society which deprived scientists of the consciousness of their social functions, thus creating in them the illusion of pure science. Accordingly, Bukharin said, the distinction between pure and applied science was inapplicable in the U.S.S.R. In his view this implied no limitation on the freedom of research; scientists could follow their interests freely in the U.S.S.R., but owing to the complete internal harmony of Socialist society they would, in actual fact, inevitably be led to lines of research which would benefit the current Five Years' Plan. And accordingly, comprehensive planning of all research was to be regarded merely as a conscious confirmation of the pre-existing harmony of scientific and social aims (SEP, 63).

As a practicing researcher, Polanyi recognized immediately that conflating pure and applied science would, if actually carried out, be fatal to pure science. In 1938, a version of this Soviet view of science was advocated in Britain when the British Association for the Advancement of Sciences founded the Division for the Social and International Relations of Science. The purpose of the new division was to provide social guidance to the progress of science. Polanyi strenuously opposed any such guidance, insisting that scientists must remain completely free to pursue their interests, inclinations, and hunches. Although pure science might make discoveries that have practical applications, its goal must always be the pursuit of knowledge for the sake of knowledge (sfs, 7).

Polanyi's travels to the Soviet Union in particular, and his encounter with oppressive political movements more generally, served to focus his mind on the justification of both science and economics. These fields are related, for both are too complex to thrive under a regimen of planning. Both science and the economy must have freedom to operate independently of externally imposed goals. Polanyi produced several books during this period. In 1935 he published *U.S.S.R. Economics*, a study detailing the systemic problems of the Soviet economy. American journalist Walter Lippmann praised the book as the work of "an exceptionally gifted observer."[13] In 1940, Polanyi published a collection of essays titled *Contempt of Freedom*, which dealt with issues of both economics and freedom of inquiry. In 1945, he released another book titled *Full Employment and Free Trade*; here he advocated a modified Keynesian approach to economic questions.

In 1944, Polanyi was elected a Fellow of the Royal Society for his scientific work. He was surprised and grateful. In a letter to Hugh O'Neill, a Manchester colleague and good friend, Polanyi reflected on the honor in terms of his own rather unsettled life: "I have been a vagabond all my life and the recognition by such a venerable body as the Royal Society does not really fit me. Perhaps I need it the more. Maybe this makes me also particularly happy in company of really settled people like yourself and Barbara, whose roots go deep into the soil of which I know only from books."[14]

At this point, as he worked to understand science and economics and to defend them from those who wished to plan their outcomes (thereby destroying that which they sought to harness), Polanyi realized that he had to address more fundamental issues. In 1945, one year after he was inducted as a Fellow of the Royal Society, Polanyi delivered the Riddell Lectures at Durham University, published the next year as *Science, Faith, and Society*. In these three lectures, Polanyi attempts to show how the practice of science—in marked contrast to the commonly accepted account—actually depends on both tradition and the authority exercised by a community of practicing scientists. Furthermore, he argues, scientists do not conduct their business in a purely explicit fashion. Instead, they rely on hunches and intuition as they seek to gain a clearer understanding of an externally existing reality, which they believe can be known. The skill of the connoisseur, then, is essential for scientific discovery to the extent that scientific knowledge is only acquired at the feet of a master. Finally, inquiry must occur within a community dedicated to such transcendent ideals as truth, justice, and charity. Only within the context of a commitment of this kind can freedom be secured, just as only in the context of a free society can the freedom of the scientist be maintained. In this 1945 lecture series, we glimpse many of the central themes that Polanyi would develop in more detail throughout the remainder of his life.

The opportunity to flesh out his views on knowledge presented itself in 1947, when he was invited to give the prestigious Gifford Lectures at the University of Aberdeen (he delivered the lectures in 1951-52). In preparing these lectures, Polanyi made the full transition from scientist to philosopher. His exuberance is clear in a letter to Arthur Koestler: "I am reading Kant's *Critique of Pure Reason* and feel grateful not to have missed this opportunity. To have lived as a scholar and missed Kant would be like visiting Egypt and missing the Pyramids."[15] To his old friend George Polya he wrote, "I have started on a study of modern logic in which I find great pleasure. It is of course rather difficult, but I have hope to achieve at least a general understanding of the position held by the thinkers of this school."[16]

It was, of course, no simple bureaucratic maneuver to formalize this change of direction. Fortunately, Polanyi had the enthusiastic backing of Manchester's vice-chancellor, Sir John Stopford. As Sir William Mansfield Cooper explains it,

> The vice-chancellor [Stopford] knew that the chance of establishing an additional chair of philosophy at that time was nil and that a dozen other chairs would rank in priority. He was aware of much American interest in Polanyi and was determined to keep him in Manchester. He was not deterred by suspicions that Polanyi could never be more, academically speaking, than an amateur philosopher. He was, in my judgement, bound to penetrate this argument. Was not Polanyi, in the strict academic

sense, an amateur in everything except his early skills in medicine? And could anyone quarrel with the result? Had one not merely to know Polanyi in an unprejudiced way to realize that here one was dealing with Erasmian man, with the protean scholar? So Stopford, without any University authority, transferred Polanyi from Chemistry to a non-existent new chair and carried the University with him. The price was doubtless the name of the chair; but 'social studies' did not really do violence to the general movement of Polanyi's interests.[17]

Thus, in 1948 Polanyi assumed the Chair of Social Studies (with limited teaching duties) and turned his full attention to nonscientific matters. As E. P. Wigner and R. A. Hodgkin describe it, "some scientific friends found the perspective that he was beginning to describe both profound and inspiring; others regretted his shift of interest and saw it as a loss to science and a darkening of reason."[18] Isaiah Berlin was not impressed: "These Hungarians are strange . . . here is a great scientist giving up the Nobel to write mediocre works of philosophy."[19] Polanyi himself, however, was quite clear about the importance of his change of tack and subsequently referred to 1946 as the year in which "I found my true vocation" as a philosopher.[20] And unlike those who lamented his turn away from science, Polanyi understood his years in the laboratory as essential preparation: "an experience in science is by far the most important basic ground for developing philosophic ideas."[21]

Polanyi delivered the Gifford Lectures in 1951 and 1952. Here, for the first time, he made the distinction between "focal" and "subsidiary" awareness that would lay at the heart of his revolutionary account of knowing. After delivering the lectures, he set about rewriting and expanding them. In 1958, *Personal Knowledge,* Polanyi's most important book, was published.

When Polanyi was preparing the Gifford Lectures in 1950, he met the American philosopher Marjorie Grene, whom he credited with "devot[ing] herself for years to the service of the present enquiry" (PK, ix). In many respects, Grene provided Polanyi with the education in philosophy that he had lacked. As a graduate student, she had attended Martin Heidegger's lectures in Freiburg and Karl Jasper's lectures in Heidelberg. She wrote her dissertation on existentialism and penned books on such diverse thinkers as Aristotle, Descartes, and Spinoza. In her 1966 book, *The Knower and the Known,* she combined Polanyi's epistemological insights with the phenomenological approach of Maurice Merleau-Ponty, discussing the implications for knowing. And in 1969, she edited a collection of Polanyi's most important essays under the title *Knowing and Being.*

After the publication of *Personal Knowledge,* Polanyi spent the rest of his career refining and extending the ideas he had developed there. In 1958, he left the University of Manchester and became a Senior Research Fellow at Merton College in Oxford. In the same year, *The Study of Man* was published; in these lectures Polanyi sought to understand the human condition in light of history. In 1962, he delivered the Terry Lectures at Yale University, a series that was published in 1966 as *The Tacit Dimension.* This work presents Polanyi's most refined explanation of his theory of tacit knowing. In the early 1970s, his health failing, Polanyi solicited the help of American philosopher Harry Prosch in assembling a series of lectures into book form. Because Polanyi, by this time, was too weak to write, Polanyi and Prosch appeared as coauthors when the book was published in 1975 under the title *Meaning*.

Polanyi's ideas never enjoyed the kind of acceptance he thought they deserved, and he felt this acutely. When he was seventy-five years old, he reflected back on the solitary road he had taken. "I was about 18 when George Polya, a fellow student a few years my senior, who was to become a great mathematician, warned mother: 'Michael walks alone, he will need a strong voice to make himself heard.' Today at 75, my voice has not yet carried far; I shall die an old man as an infant prodigy."[22] Polanyi often wondered why his ideas were not greeted with more enthusiasm. One possible reason is that Polanyi's approach to philosophy was simply beyond the strictures of analytic philosophy. His ideas, therefore, would have been largely invisible to professional philosophers in Britain. Polanyi found few allies at Oxford, that seedbed of positivism and linguistic philosophy where such influential figures such A. J. Ayer and Gilbert Ryle cast long shadows. Because he usually found more appreciative audiences in the United States, Polanyi frequently traveled and lectured there. He held visiting positions at several universities in the United States, including Wesleyan, Stanford, Duke, Virginia, the University of Texas at Austin, and the University of Chicago. At the same time, philosopher of science Rom Harré, an Oxford colleague who took Polanyi's work seriously, saw things differently. In a 1967 letter, he wrote: "I have always thought, Michael, that your work lives right in the British tradition. . . . One day I shall persuade you that you are not a lone hand but a member of what is to me a great tradition."[23]

Michael Polanyi's extraordinary life ended peacefully in Oxford on February 22, 1976. In a way, he was a contemporary Renaissance man, for during his lengthy intellectual career he made important contributions to a number of very different fields of study. In the following chapters, we will get some sense of his thinking in economics, the practice of science, politics, philosophy, and religion, but we should always keep in mind that the first half of his life was devoted almost exclusively to chemistry. Apart from the two political essays he published as a young man in Hungary, he did not begin publishing nonscientific articles until 1935, when he was in his mid-forties. And when the University of Manchester switched his chair from physical chemistry to social studies in 1948, Polanyi was fifty-seven years old. At a time many people are well-established in a particular field and perhaps content to rest on their past achievements, Polanyi was in the early stages of formulating an account of knowledge that was, quite simply, revolutionary—one that provided a way out of the dilemma philosophy had encountered. Confronted with the alternatives of Enlightenment rationalism (which has clearly failed to live up to its promises) and what has come to be called postmodernism, Polanyi's theory of knowledge neither succumbs to rationalist hubris nor retreats into the hovel of postmodern despair. While Polanyi explored a wide variety of nonscientific fields, all find a fundamental unity in his account of knowing, or what he called personal knowledge.

CHAPTER TWO

ECONOMICS, SCIENCE, AND POLITICS

Economics

For those living in the post-Soviet era, it is easy to forget that the merits of a planned economy were once hotly debated and that many intellectuals were convinced that some form of socialism would eventually prevail over free-market economic systems. Polanyi was a vocal and energetic opponent of command economies, and he wrote extensively on this topic. In 1935, he published an essay titled "Soviet Economics—Fact and Theory." Here, he sought to show quantitatively that this economy based on communist ideology had failed to create the kind of wealth that the party leaders had promised. Starting in the 1930s, Polanyi wrote on economic issues for some three decades.

According to Polanyi, there are only two imaginable ways of arranging economic systems: either some form of a market system or some form of centralized planning. Polanyi resolved the dilemma in unequivocal terms: "I affirm that the central planning of production . . . is strictly impossible" (LL, 136). Therefore, Polanyi could assert with confidence, "there exists no radical alternative to the capitalist system" (LL, 170). The fatal impediment to a centralized economy is the fact of human finitude. A centralized system (or what overconfident advocates might call "scientific planning") is predicated on the belief that the central authority is capable of gathering and assimilating all available information about every aspect of the economic system and then making decisions based upon that information. Yet there is an obvious problem with this belief: "the central authority, however properly constituted it may be as a government, is in fact ignorant of the desires of its constituents as far as their day-to-day wants are concerned" (SEP, 148). In short, any complex economic system possesses multiple centers; a single center can never completely and accurately represent the desires and needs of the various players. This apparently insurmountable problem of centralization is rooted in what Polanyi calls "polycentricity."

To address economic questions adequately in Polanyi's view, one must employ a polycentric approach rather than a centralized one. A polycentric system is one that operates according to the mutually adjusting actions of independent participants. The coordination or order that ensues is not commanded from the top, but is what Polanyi calls a "spontaneous order" (a term Austrian economist Friedrich von Hayek would later adopt from Polanyi[1]). Polanyi argues that, wherever complexity exists, the same principle will apply. "It applies even to a sack of potatoes. Consider how ingeniously the knobs of each potato fit into the hollows of a neighbor. Weeks of careful planning by a team of engineers equipped with a complete set of cross-sections for each potato would not reduce the total volume filled by the potatoes in the sack so effectively as a good shaking and a few kicks will do." This is even more evident when we turn to human relations. For example, "take a soccer team of eleven mutually adjusting at every moment their play to each other, and pit it against a team each member of which has to wait before making a move for the orders of a captain controlling the players by radio. Central direction would spell paralysis" (SEP, 168).

Turning specifically to economics, Polanyi identifies three separate but related polycentric problems. First, there is the problem of distributing goods to consumers. Each person has different needs and desires; each will rank different goods in a different order of preference, and each will be willing to pay different prices for the same good. Second, there is the problem of using various resources in order to produce goods. A central authority cannot adequately dictate to a manager how much raw materials, labor, machinery, etc., will be required to make X amount of a particular product. The quality of the materials, the skill of the labor, and the type of machinery will all affect the outcome, and the manager will necessarily have to respond to these variations with individual adjustments that could not have been anticipated and dictated by a central authority. The third polycentric problem is that of the investment of capital. The investor, if he is to stay in business, will have to assess accurately the merits of various projects. Again, this can only be accomplished on an individual level (SEP, 152–53).

If economic systems are in fact polycentric, it would follow that any attempt to institute a truly centralized economy is doomed to fail. Polanyi saw the Soviet attempt to implement a command economy as a clear vindication of his argument:

> The early phase of the Russian Revolution thus presents an experiment, as clear as history is ever likely to provide, in which (1) Socialist economic planning was pressed home; (2) this had eventually to be abandoned on the grounds that the measures adopted had caused an unparalleled economic disaster; and (3) the abandonment of the Socialist measures and the restoration of capitalist methods of production retrieved economic life from disaster and set it on the road to rapid recovery (LL, 163).

Polanyi pointed out that, despite the rhetoric coming from the Communist Party, "communism broke down in the famine and was repealed by Lenin in March, 1921. In 1921 Russia largely returned to private capitalism. The New Economic Policy left all but the main industries to private persons, thus restricting itself to a direct control of about 10 per cent of production" (CF, 62). Polanyi distinguishes here between pure communism, which seeks to abolish the entire market mechanism, and socialism, which relies fundamentally upon the market despite government ownership of major industries. In order to prevent a repeat of the disaster of 1921, the preferred course was clear: "Publicly owned enterprises must therefore operate through a market even though this may be heavily overlaid by a pretense of central direction" (SEP, 171). What was called planning in the Soviet economy, then, was really something far different. "The target of the next two or three months is fixed by adding to the results of the last period a small percentage of expansion" (SEP, 177). But merely demanding that each sector expand gradually is hardly an example of the sort of scientific planning of which the Communist Party boasted. Polanyi calls its bluff. "This is not central direction but a ubiquitous central pressure, which forces enterprises to operate constantly to the limits of their capacity and to widen this capacity from quarter to quarter by a process of trial and error" (SEP, 178).

Polanyi was a fierce opponent of collectivism, but he was no *laissez-faire* libertarian. On the contrary, he accused both libertarians and collectivists of being wrongly suspicious of government intervention in economic matters:

> The orthodox Liberals maintain that, if the market is limited by the fixation of some of its elements, then it must cease to function, the implication being that there exists a logical system of complete *laissez faire*, the only rational alternative to which is collectivism. That is precisely the position which collectivists want us to take up when asserting that none of the evils of the market can be alleviated except by destroying the whole institution root and branch (SEP, 140).

As we saw above, Polanyi was convinced that there are only two conceivable economic arrangements and that one of them, collectivism, is inherently defective. Capitalism is the only viable option, but this does not imply that the state has no role beyond enforcing contracts and preventing fraud. On the contrary, the state can work (albeit at the margins) to ensure that the market operates as effectively as possible. As he put it, "while the State must continue to canalize, correct and supplement the forces of the market, it cannot replace them to any considerable extent" (LL, 171).

Because he had served in the Austro-Hungarian army, Polanyi was not allowed to work on top-secret projects in England during

World War II. Yet he was determined to contribute to what he believed was a fundamental struggle for liberty. He became convinced that his task was to articulate the foundations upon which a free society operates, and he sought ways to take his insights beyond the confines of the academy. In 1938, Polanyi produced the first part of an animated film illustrating the money cycle. Professor Henry Clay, an economic advisor to the Bank of England, was impressed:

> The fact that his interest in economics is not professional enables him to approach the problems of presentation in a way that would be almost impossible for a professional economist. . . . He is a much better economist already than most professional economists, and, if he is able to give a part of his mind to economics, he is much more likely to make an effective contribution than nine out of ten of the people who hold chairs in economics in the Universities.[2]

Polanyi and others showed the film to a variety of audiences in an attempt to educate the public on the basics of economic theory, but the film did not generate the grand results Polanyi had hoped for. In 1945, Cambridge University Press published Polanyi's *Full Employment and Free Trade,* in which he attempted to synthesize Keynesian and monetarist economics. At the time, the field of economics was dominated by the thought of John Maynard Keynes, whose landmark book *General Theory of Employment, Interest, and Money* (1936) had seemingly established the irrelevance of the monetarist approach. The title of Polanyi's book suggests its thrust: contrary to traditional Keynesian views, Polanyi thought it was possible to attain full employment within the context of a free (unplanned) economy. As he put it in a letter to Karl Mannheim, "I think I represent among my friends the most 'radical' Keynesian attitude which—incidentally—involves the least planning."[3] Paul Craig Roberts (one of Polanyi's last graduate students) and Norman Van Cott suggest that, because Polanyi was not formally trained as an economist, he was able to avoid becoming entangled in some of the pivotal errors into which professional economists had fallen.[4]

Polanyi focused on the primacy of the money supply. As he puts it, "this book is largely concerned with tracing the channels through which money is brought into circulation or withdrawn from circulation" (FEFT, 8). Using several illustrations taken from the animated film, Polanyi shows how the "money belt," when properly balanced, will produce the condition of full employment. On the other hand, if the amount of money constricts, depression will result, while an excess of money will produce inflation. According to Polanyi, two forces impact the money supply: savings, which reduce the supply, and investment, which increases it.

A central concern of economists at the time was to explain the world crisis that had struck in the 1930s. Depression and unemployment had to be understood so that future crises could be averted. According to the Keynesians, unemployment is caused by depressed demand; the solution is for government to increase demand through deficit spending. On the other hand, Polanyi argued, as Milton Friedman would years later, that unemployment results from insufficient money. According to Polanyi, government could inject money into the economy until full employment was achieved. If money continued flowing in after that point, inflation would occur, and the value of money would decrease. As Roberts and Van

Cott put it, "Polanyi synthesized Keynesian economics with the monetary school of economics later associated with Milton Friedman. In this synthesis, Polanyi was at least two decades, and perhaps three, ahead of the best minds in the economics profession."[5]

Curiously, this book received scant attention, even though it was published by one of the premier academic publishing houses in the world. In the 1940s, strong currents opposed the ideas Polanyi advocated. Where not only Keynesians but also socialists of various stripes dominated the debates, there was little audience for Polanyi's ideas. According to Roberts and Van Cott,

> He was too far ahead of his time and too far outside his bailiwick. Had he possessed an economics chair and graduate students, he might have been in contention as the most important economist of his time, eclipsing both Keynes and Friedman by his early synthesis. Economics and public policy would have been spared the long and pointless Keynesian odyssey toward big government.[6]

As we have seen, Polanyi was neither an advocate of *laissez-faire* policies nor of central planning. His former colleague John Jewkes notes this moderate tack of Polanyi's economic thought:

> Running through all his writings in economics, there seems to be one central strand: how best to reconcile the safeguarding of individual liberty with the controls upon the individual inseparable from a complex and organized society, or as Polanyi succinctly put it, the relation between spontaneous and social order. His analysis was pointing not only to the inhumanities of totalitarianism but also to the muddle and drift which so often result from overconfident planning in freer societies.[7]

In 1944, the year before the publication of *Full Employment and Free Trade*, Michael's brother Karl published his most important book, *The Great Transformation*. Born in 1886, Karl was five years Michael's senior. As a student at the University of Budapest, Karl was the first president of the Galileo Circle, the radical student organization to which Michael also belonged. Like many in that group, Karl saw socialism as the remedy for the ills spawned by societies that had succumbed to the demands of the free market. Fellow Hungarian Paul Ignotus writes of Karl, "I am inclined to pay him the tribute of calling him the most left-handed politician I have ever come across."[8] During the First World War, Karl, like his brother, served in the Austro-Hungarian army. After the war, he settled for some years in Vienna, where he worked as a senior editor of a left-leaning weekly news magazine, *Der Österreichische Volkswirt*. It was during this time that he first encountered the work of Ludwig von Mises and his most famous student Friedrich von Hayek. Mises and Hayek were the intellectual fathers of a movement that did not become fully visible until decades later. As advocates of market liberalism in the mid-twentieth century, dominated as it was by Keynesians and socialists, theirs were lonely voices. And Karl Polanyi was convinced they were terribly wrong.

In 1933, because his socialist leanings were not viewed favorably by Hitler's new government, Karl was forced to resign his position. He left Vienna for Britain, where he worked as a lecturer for the Workers' Educational Association, the extramural outreach arm of the universities of Oxford and London. In 1941, he began a two-year term as a visiting scholar at Bennington College in Vermont.

It was during his time at Bennington that he wrote the bulk of *The Great Transformation*, a book of economic and social history that sought to illuminate the woeful social effects of market liberalism. Coincidentally, Karl's book was published in the same year as Hayek's influential book *The Road to Serfdom,* a work that sought to make a case quite the opposite of Karl's.

Karl Polanyi's thesis is straight forward: "The idea of a self-adjusting market implied a stark utopia."

> Such an institution could not exist for any length of time without annihilating the human and natural substance of society; it would have physically destroyed man and transformed his surroundings into a wilderness. Inevitably, society took measures to protect itself, but whatever measures it took impaired the self-regulation of the market, disorganized industrial life, and thus endangered society in yet another way.[9]

According to Karl, a market economy can only exist within a market society; thus, the institution of a market economy fundamentally altered the structure of society. Whereas prior economies were embedded within a larger social framework, the rise of the industrial market economy essentially reversed this relationship. Thus, "instead of economy being embedded in social relations, social relations are embedded in the economic system."[10] The result of this shift was a commodification of things that were never previously looked upon as commodities: namely, land, labor, and money. On the one hand, "to separate labor from other activities of life and to subject it to the laws of the market was to annihilate all organic forms of existence and to replace them by a different type of organization, an atomistic and individualistic one."[11] As a result, all human relations came to be understood under the rubric of freedom of contract. On the other hand, land "is an element of nature inextricably interwoven with man's institutions. To isolate it and form a market for it was perhaps the weirdest of all the undertakings of our ancestors."[12] In short, land and labor are fundamental components of every complex human society; "to include them in the market mechanism means to subordinate the substance of society itself to the laws of the market."[13]

This "stark utopia" that is the self-regulating market came to represent a sort of "secular salvation."[14] But as a utopia, this new hope for humanity was doomed to fail. The social destruction that a pure market economy would have produced was intolerable even to the most ardent advocates of the market. Thus, said Karl, we see a "double movement" in which, on the one hand, we hear calls for freeing the market from any nonmarket restraints; yet we also hear a contrary call for restraints on the market to prevent or correct its failures. This, according to Karl, is proof that a self-regulating market simply cannot work. Intervention is inevitable if the complete dissolution of society is to be avoided.

Karl Polanyi looked to socialism as a viable alternative to a market economy. "Socialism," he writes, "is, essentially, the tendency inherent in an industrial civilization to transcend the self-regulating market by consciously subordinating it to a democratic society."[15] For Karl, the problem was not industrialization *per se* but the dream of a market society. "Industrial civilization will continue to exist when the utopian experiment of a self-regulating market will be no more than a memory."[16] He looked to the example of the Soviet Union after its brief and disastrous flirtation with pure communism in the early 1920s as a model "which proved an amazing success."[17]

Karl confidently predicted a future that moved beyond the false promises of the self-regulating market. Future societies might be arranged in various ways, including democratic, aristocratic, constitutional, and authoritarian, "but the outcome is common with them all: the market system will no longer be self-regulating, even in principle, since it will not comprise labor, land, and money."[18] He did not suggest that future societies would include no role for the market. Instead, he argued that markets must be properly conceived in the context of the societies of which they are only a part. Once land, labor, and money were freed from the constraints of the market, markets would be rightly understood as tools to enhance human societies rather than the essential basis around which a society must be formed. In short, society is primary; markets are not. Karl Polanyi concludes his book with these words:

> Uncomplaining acceptance of the reality of society gives man indomitable courage and strength to remove all removable injustices and unfreedom. As long as he is true to his task of creating more abundant freedom for all, he need not fear that either power or planning will turn against him and destroy the freedom he is building by their instrumentality. This is the meaning of freedom in a complex society; it gives us all the certainty that we need.[19]

On some very basic economic and political questions, then, Michael Polanyi found himself at odds with his brother. First, they disagreed about the Soviet Union. Shortly after the appearance of Michael's 1935 publication titled *U.S.S.R. Economics: Fact and Theory*, Karl wrote to his brother: "I am still completely baffled by the almost complete lack of human meaning and significance of your booklet."[20] While he was critical of much that occurred in the Soviet Union, Karl Polanyi remained optimistic that the Soviet experiment could one day bring about the social and economic reforms he desired. Michael, on the other hand, was under no such illusions. His visits to the Soviet Union and his contact with dissidents, together with his intellectual commitment to liberty, motivated his long struggle against totalitarianism. With his fellow countryman and ex-communist Arthur Koestler, Polanyi was active in the leadership of the Congress for Cultural Freedom, an organization dedicated to fighting communism and extending intellectual freedom throughout the world.

Second, Michael Polanyi advocated a policy of governmental neutrality. As he put it in *Full Employment and Free Trade*, "I maintain that a policy of Full Employment can be conducted separately, on its own merits: and must therefore be so conducted. The principle of neutrality which I have advocated in this connection is but a variant of the principle of separation of economics from politics" (FEFT, 135–36). Polanyi's reason for this separation was rooted in his perception of a need for accountability.

> If each organ of society were allowed to regard the public interest always as a whole, unrestrained by any specific references or rules, there would be no criterion by which any matter could be traced to any particular agent or any agent be called upon to

give an account of his specific functions. Only under a clear
division of competences and by subjection to definite rules, therefore, can the management of society be conducted responsibly;
and only in these conditions can public opinion scrutinize and
guide the functions of Government (FEF1, 135).

Karl Polanyi recognized that when Michael called for a separation
of economics and politics, his target was a central idea in *The
Great Transformation*. He wrote his brother: "The separation of
politics and economics is not the charge leveled by 'Marxian'
socialism against a market economy, but it is mainly my non-
Marxian formulation of the characteristic of nineteenth-century
society."[21]

Their respective views on the nature of political power represent another important difference between the Polanyi brothers.
Michael perceived that consolidated power held without accountability invites abuse. This abuse can take an overt form characterized by violence, or it can manifest itself in the *hubris* that attempts to institute a centrally planned system. In the final paragraph of his *The Great Transformation*, by contrast, Karl argues
that we have no reason to fear either power or planning. Michael's
central argument against the possibility of planning was that it is
simply impossible. Polycentric systems cannot be planned centrally. Thus, while Karl insisted that a self-regulated market
economy is a utopian dream, his brother argued that the real
fantasy is the idea that a complex economy can be conducted
according to a central plan. Michael agreed with his brother that
there is a positive and necessary role for government in maintain-

ing the health of the economy. Yet he was not critical of the free market *per se*, nor did he seem disturbed by the inclusion of land and labor in the market system.

Perhaps the most fundamental difference lies in their respective accounts of the cause of the current crisis. As we have seen, Karl suggested—and here we can identify Marx's influence on his thought—that the woes of the twentieth century resulted from a faulty economic structure. These obstacles could be overcome if the right institutions were altered better to reflect human nature. Yet Michael, as we will see, ultimately located the problem in the spiritual and moral vacuum that resulted from a deficient conception of knowing—one that denied the very possibility of spiritual and moral reality. This denial was the product of a view of reality that was both skeptical and materialistic. Michael Polanyi called this union "objectivism." Because we cannot adequately grasp his concerns without first understanding what he means by this term, we will now explore this idea in the context of science.

Science

Polanyi employs the concept of spontaneous order to describe not only economic and social relations but the activities of scientists as well. That he was compelled to defend the liberty of the scientist in the same fashion that he was compelled to defend economic and social liberty indicates the pervasive nature of the centralizing ideology of the mid-twentieth century. This ideology, as communist and Marxist literature makes abundantly clear, was rooted in a materialistic vision of the world, a world conceieved completely in terms of cause-and-effect relationships. It was possible, then, to imagine controlling this causal mechanism from a centralized position, thus rendering the entire system more (if not perfectly) efficient. Even those not motivated explicitly by a commitment to Marxism came increasingly to hold that all knowledge worthy of the name is explicitly verifiable. Whatever could not be verified on purely empirical or logical grounds could not justifiably be called knowledge. Polanyi traces what came to be called positivism back to the early modern period, which was characterized by an explicit and categorical rejection of the authority of the Aristotelian and religious traditions. Those traditions were seen as oppressive and as hindrances to the pursuit of truth. Any reliance on belief or tradition as a starting point for investigation was rejected—an idea that still has purchase today. Polanyi writes:

> To assert any belief uncritically has come to be regarded as an offence against reason. We feel in it the danger of obscurantism and the menace of an arbitrary restriction of free thought. Against these evils of dogmatism we protect ourselves by upholding the principle of doubt which rejects any open affirmation of faith (SB, 217).[22]

The twin streams of early modern philosophy—rationalism and empiricism—both rejected any dependence on tradition and authority. As Polanyi puts it, "Cartesian doubt and Locke's empiricism . . . had the purpose of demonstrating that truth could be established and a rich and satisfying doctrine of man and the universe built up on the foundations of critical reason alone" (SFS, 75).[23] Polanyi argues that the descendants of Descartes and Locke still pursued their ideals in the twentieth century; these ideals manifested themselves in the forms of both logical positivism and skepticism. Modern empiricists and skeptics "are all convinced that our main troubles still come from our having not altogether rid ourselves of all traditional beliefs and continue to set their hopes on further applications of the method of radical scepticism and empiricism" (SFS, 76). Polanyi's friend Arthur Koestler aptly described those who reject all reference to the past as "men born without umbilical cords."[24]

The attempt to reject all dependence on tradition and authority (which implies belief) gave rise to the ideal of explicit, objective knowledge. Tradition and authority are mediating elements that inevitably influence the mind subjected to them. It was assumed that a mind subjected to such influences cannot obtain the necessary distance to attain a purely objective and explicit grasp of the facts. Thus, the war on tradition is the attempt to rid the mind of epistemological mediaries that cloud and influence the mind and prevent the knower from accessing unmediated truth. According to Polanyi, "objectivism has totally falsified our conception of truth, by exalting what we can know and prove, while covering up with ambiguous utterances all we can know and *cannot* prove, even though the latter knowledge underlies, and must ultimately set its seal to, all that we *can* prove" (PK, 286). The demand for explicit and verifiable grounds for making truth claims necessarily leads to skepticism about the very things we once held most dear. This sort of skepticism carries with it a materialistic view of reality, for the empiricism that underwrites objectivism refuses to grant the status of "truth" to anything that is not empirically verifiable.

While such rigor might initially suggest a fidelity to the strict canons of the scientific method, this is not actually the case. As Polanyi points out with great frequency, the picture of the scientist setting aside all personal prejudices and following the evidence in a purely impersonal and dispassionate fashion is simply an illusion.[25] In addition to the personal nature of the scientific enterprise, the process of discovery necessarily includes unaccountable elements, elements that simply cannot be rendered in purely explicit terms. Polanyi likes to refer to Kant, that paragon of rigorous thought, who noted that no system of rules prescribes when and how a particular rule is to be applied. By way of explanation, Kant recurred to the less-than-precise notion of "mother wit." When he considers the way human minds arrange particulars as members of separate classes, Kant refers to "a skill so deeply hidden in the human soul that we shall hardly guess the secret trick that Nature here employs" (KB, 105). Such things as "mother wit" and "a secret trick" appear to be two ways of intimating that at the root of knowing lie powers that simply defy specification. Polanyi notes that a critique of pure reason is surely deficient if it fails to account for such powers and merely passes them by with a few quick and scattered sentences. That Kant did not attend to this problem is instructive:

> Perhaps both Kant and his successors instinctively preferred to let such sleeping monsters lie, for fear that, once awakened, they might destroy their fundamental conception of knowledge. For, once you face up to the ubiquitous controlling position of unformalizable mental skills, you do meet difficulties for the justification of knowledge that cannot be disposed of within the framework of rationalism (KB, 106).

When a scientist (or anyone else for that matter) seeks to solve a problem, he attempts to assess the relevant information and then to make a guess about the aspect of reality upon which the information bears. For any problem, there are an infinite number of possible explanations; but few solutions—or perhaps only one—produce a coherent account. How does the scientist sift through the possibilities and settle on the solution? If he were required to make a list of every possible solution and then test each one systematically, he would spend a lifetime on one or at most a few simple problems. In reality, the scientist eliminates the vast majority of possible solutions without testing them. How does he do this?

The general view of scientific inquiry is the scientific method we all learned in grade school: we form a hypothesis and then test it. Polanyi rejects this conception of science. Instead, "all true scientific research starts with hitting on a deep and promising problem, and this is half the discovery." A problem is not a hypothesis; "it is something much vaguer." In this regard, consider the following dilemma: "Supposing the discovery of a problem were replaced by the setting up of a hypothesis . . . such a hypothesis would have to be either one formulated at random or so chosen that it has a fair initial chance to be true. If the former, its chances of proving true would be negligible; if the latter, we are left with the question how it is arrived at" (KB, 118–19). Thus, a scientist must have the ability to see a problem. Far from being fully specifiable, this ability "relies on largely unspecifiable clues which can be sensed, mobilized and integrated only by a passionate response to their hidden meaning" (KB, 118). Polanyi calls this skill intuition, but he notes that this is not some mystical ability.

Rather, it is quite similar to perception. When we attempt to perceive an object, we concentrate and perhaps even squint in order better to bring the object into focus. In the same way, this unspecifiable element called intuition "is a skill, rooted in our natural sensibility to hidden patterns and developed to effectiveness by a process of learning" (KB, 118). Thus, quite contrary to the standard image of a dispassionate scientist, Polanyi argues that the scientist relies on his personal passions as well as the skill of intuition—both of which are not fully explicable. Without these concepts, it is impossible to provide an account of science that adequately reflects actual scientific practice.

As we saw in the last chapter, Polanyi was deeply affected by his conversation with Bukharin in 1935. He recognized an important challenge to the way science had traditionally been viewed. If there is no difference between pure science and practical science, then the scientist must necessarily plan his activities around the perceived needs of the society of which he is a part. In other words, he must identify a practical problem (or the problem can be identified for him by the Party) and then he must marshal his scientific resources in the pursuit of a solution. Science, thus conceived, becomes a tool that serves the economy or society at large. The assumption that the scientist must have the autonomy to pursue his own individual interests without any concern whatsoever for the social or economic application of his findings is considered a luxury at best. More probably, it is regarded as a wasteful consumption of resources, one that reveals the narcissism of the scientist who engages in such esoteric activities.

Notably, this attitude was not confined to the Soviet Union. While there were no Five-Year Plans in Britain, there was, in some circles, sympathy for the ideals of communism. Some intellectuals made a significant impact on the debate with books that denied the idea that science should be pursued for the sake of enlightenment pure and simple. Books such as J. G. Crowther's *Social Relations of Science* and J. D. Bernal's *The Social Function of Science* sought to convince the public that science must be put to work for the benefit of the society. (This view was, of course, significantly aided by the very real pressures to mobilize British society for war). By 1945, Polanyi could write that "it has in fact become rare to find any public statement today which would declare it clearly that the main purpose of science is the acquisition of knowledge for its own sake" (LL, 84). While he goes on to admit that most scientists still hold this older view, the general public, he was convinced, did not. Polanyi could see that this boded ill for the future of science.

That Polanyi was concerned about the public pereception of science reveals an important insight that he gained through experience. Scientists necessarily conduct their work in the context of society as a whole. If scientists desire to be free to pursue their research for the sake of knowledge itself, they must retain the favorable opinion of the public, for many if not most scientists conduct their research using public money. When the public shifts its view of science, scientists cannot blithely continue with their research as if nothing has changed. As Polanyi could see only too well, if the public embraced a purely functional view of science, the scientist would be co-opted to serve the chosen ends of society. Rather than being free to follow his own interests and hunches, the scientist would be compelled to submit his interests and goals to those of the society or party. Thus, Polanyi recognized both the scientist's tenuous position as well as his corresponding responsibility to move, when necessary, beyond the laboratory in order to protect science against those who would co-opt it and thereby fundamentally change it.

Clearly, the argument embraced by those who sought to conflate pure science and applied science rests on a sort of moral imperative. In a review of J. D. Bernal's *The Social Function of Science*, Polanyi notes that the "ruling passion" of those who deny the intrinsic good of pure science is "a profound resentment of delays in the achievement of plenitude, health and enlightenment to which, he believes, science even now holds the door open" (SEP, 61). Such a sentiment may appear noble, but as Polanyi argues, successfully reducing all science to applied science—that is, to research with immediate and obvious practical applications—would in effect signal the end of science as we know it.

In order for science to be oriented exclusively toward achieving practical results, one would have first to establish clear goals for scientific research. These goals would, of course, have to be constructed in light of those current problems which seem most eligible for attention. Take cancer research as an example. Curing cancer is surely a worthy endeavor. Imagine if the attention of scientists were universally turned to developing such a cure: the talent and resources now "squandered" on endeavors that yield nothing save the satisfaction of understanding a little more about our world would be diverted to the concrete goal of eradicating a terrible disease. The problem with this plan, according to Polanyi,

is that it would not work. "For all its practical interest, knowledge of cancer can only advance if and when the progress of physiology, biochemistry, cytology, and other branches of science does
throw from time to time new light on one or other of its aspects.
. . . Moreover, all such progress is wholly derived from the freedom of the systematic branches of science to pursue their own
specific scientific aims" (SEP, 66). This is not to say that practical
applications cannot and do not emerge from the pursuit of pure
science. But the practical results are "merely incidental to the over-
riding purpose of advancing knowledge" (LL, 90). In this sense,
Polanyi's view of pure science as the pursuit of knowledge for its
own sake echoes John Henry Newman's defense of liberal education in *The Idea of a University*.[26]

Science conceived in this light is the open-ended attempt to
understand reality. But because individual scientists pursue projects
they have freely chosen in the manner they think best, the growth
of science is unpredictable. "To illustrate the growth of science we
must imagine a statue which, while it is being pieced together,
appears complete at every successive stage." But if we look back at
the development of science over the centuries, it becomes clear
that there have been many surprise discoveries that, in essence,
have radically altered the shape of the statue. One need only think
of the shift from Ptolemy to Copernicus, or from Newton to
Einstein. As Polanyi argues, the statue "would . . . appear to change
its meaning on the addition of every successive fragment—to the
great and ever renewed surprise of the bystanders" (LL, 110).

One of the problems with planning science, then, is that
no one can anticipate discoveries in advance of the discoveries

themselves. A related problem is one of information. If a central authority proposed to direct the goals of science for whatever purpose, the goals would have to be established in light of the current status of science. But determining that status is no simple task—for two reasons. First, in order to make a credible statement about the current status of science, one would have to absorb and assimilate the untold number of books and journals dedicated to the advancement of science. Such a capacity is beyond any one individual or centralized authority. Second, even assuming the information could be collected, "no one has yet been able to obtain from it a comprehensive conception of the position of science, nor any idea as to the direction in which it should advance as a whole." Speaking with the authority of one who had practiced pure science for years, Polanyi recognized that speaking of the progress of science as a whole was the kind of meaningless nonsense that only a nonscientist could utter. "It is of the essence of science, in contrast to scholastic speculation, that it advances piecemeal, by extending knowledge wherever discoveries can be made and not with reference to a central problem" (SEP, 132).

But if the elimination of pure science in favor of planned, practical science is a hopelessly impossible aspiration, how should science be conducted? We have already seen suggestions that the individual scientist should be free to pursue the problems he deems important and interesting; but does this mean that the pursuit of scientific knowledge is merely an anarchical enterprise? If this were so, how could good science be distinguished from bad? Polanyi addresses this by noting the difference between planning and supervision. Science cannot be planned—this we have seen. But it can and must be supervised, for without supervision, science would be forced to admit into its ranks such pursuits as astrology, witchcraft, and water divining.

Planning, by definition, entails a central authority that initiates and directs the actions of all practitioners in a vertical command structure. Supervision proceeds on quite different terms:

> Supervision presupposes human activities which are initiated from a great multitude of centres, and it aims at regulating these manifold impulses in conformity with their inherent purpose. It achieves this by making generally available social machinery and other regulated opportunities for independent action, and . by letting all the individual agents interact through a medium of freely circulating ideas and information (SEP, 127).

Polanyi likens the development of science to the cultivation of chess. Chess organizations develop a uniform set of rules, arrange tournaments, keep records of the performance of individual players, record and make available past games for study, etc. In short, the organization works in a variety of ways to advance the understanding of chess. Nevertheless, a chess organization would never dream of dictating moves to individual players during their matches. Like individual scientists, each chess player pursues his goal according to his own inclinations and abilities—with the underlying condition that he remain within the rules established by the chess organization (SEP, 128; LL, 42).

This ideal of coupling a supervision of science with a free and fluid dissemination of information can occur only in a liberal society, where information-sharing is encouraged. But here, Polanyi distinguishes between a free society and a completely open or permissive one. The kind of society Polanyi describes is not one in which individuals are at liberty to do anything they please so long as they do not infringe upon any other individual's freedom to do the same. This is an inadequate foundation to support the supervisory structure required for the continuation of either science or a free society. A free society voluntarily and necessarily upholds an orthodoxy, but in upholding an orthodoxy, some positions are necessarily excluded. A free society champions the belief that "man is amenable to reason and susceptible to the claims of his conscience" (LL, 35). Furthermore, a free society must be a good society, "a body of men who respect truth, desire justice and love their fellows" (LL, 36). Belief in such "transcendent ideals" as truth, justice, and charity are necessary for the perpetuation of society as a whole and the sustenance of science in particular. "The totalitarian form of the State arises logically from the denial of reality to this realm of transcendent ideals" (LL, 57). In other words, for Polanyi, the open society that denies any orthodoxy, that denies any necessary and corporate commitment to certain transcendent ideals, has nothing to protect itself from the rise of totalitarianism. The demise of both political liberty and science can only be resisted by a commitment to "the whole spiritual realm of truth, justice, humaneness, beauty and their organisations in the forms of laws, politics, moral customs, arts, religion. The same reasons which cause science to be paralysed by any imposition of secular authority makes all the wealth of this realm turn to dust the moment it is made subject to the demands of the State" (SEP, 67).

Polanyi reiterates this same distinction in an essay on academic freedom when he distinguishes between two kinds of freedom. The first kind is, perhaps, the one that comes to mind when we first consider the topic. It is freedom from any external constraint. Polanyi associates this conception of freedom with utilitarianism. He argues that such a view of freedom is inadequate, for "this individualist or self-assertive conception of freedom can, unfortunately, be used to justify all kinds of objectionable behaviour. At some time or other it has been invoked in protection of the worst forms of exploitation, even the keeping of slaves. . . . Its fundamental opposition to all restraint can easily be turned into nihilism" (LL, 40). A second kind of freedom, Polanyi argues, is virtually the opposite of the first. "It regards freedom as liberation from personal ends by submission to impersonal obligations. Its prototype is Luther facing the hostile Assembly at Worms with the words 'Hier stehe ich und kann nicht anders.'" But as with the first conception of freedom, this second form can be abused, for in one sense it appears quite similar to totalitarianism. "It does become altogether totalitarian if you regard the State as the supreme guardian of the public good; for it then follows that the individual is made free by surrendering completely to the State" (LL, 40). While these two conceptions of freedom are important elements in a fully articulated account of freedom, both require careful cultivation, for one can totter into nihilism while the other can fall headlong into totalitarianism.

In order to insulate the first form of freedom from nihilism, some form of authority is necessary. In the context of the practice of science (or any other academic discipline), an excess of the first kind of freedom would lead to chaos and disarray within the discipline. If each practitioner were allowed to pursue whatever projects he deemed fit and then given equal space in the professional journals with every other member of the discipline, there would be no mechanism by which to determine what distinguishes the good from the bad, the master from the charlatan. Polanyi frequently employed a memorable example to illustrate his point. In the 1940 issue of the journal *Nature*, a graph was published demonstrating that the gestation period of a number of animals is a multiple of the number π. Against this, Polanyi argued that no scientist, regardless of the evidence that could be marshaled, could be convinced that the relationship is anything but a coincidence. So too with the predictions of astrology: though some practitioners might make predictions with uncanny accuracy, Polanyi notes, no scientist would recognize this as anything but chance (LL, 20).

Why the skepticism? Because in the same way that a free society (as opposed to an open one) is necessarily rooted in a commitment to an orthodoxy, so too, the individual academic disciplines are organized and sustained by similar commitments. The practice of science occurs within the context of certain rules. Science is supervised by players who have agreed to play by rules they themselves have created. A scientist, then, cannot be a scientist in isolation. Granted, his particular circumstances may force him into physical isolation (as with scientists in a totalitarian regime); but he can only practice science by willingly submitting to the authority of the scientific community. His work will only be considered science if it operates according to the orthodoxy that the scientific community has voluntarily established for itself. Standards of rationality, fidelity to truth, and a commitment to some form of naturalistic explanations of phenomena are all part of the set of beliefs or rules to which the scientist willingly adheres. Thus, nihilism is avoided only when individual scientists submit themselves to this authority of their own creation and tailor their work and interests to the strictures that have been established by that authority.

The second conception of freedom can be corrupted as well. Science is, Polanyi argues, a cooperative enterprise supervised but not planned. Yet such cooperation implies that each practitioner is committed not only to playing by the same rules that bind the others, but also to the belief that all are pursuing the same ultimate ends. Polanyi asks us to imagine a large jigsaw puzzle that would take one person days or weeks to complete. What would be the most effective way to solve the puzzle? Would it be best for a central planner to duplicate the pieces of the puzzle and then send out the duplicate puzzles to a variety of teams? This would not speed the task appreciably, for each group would necessarily repeat the work of every other group. Polanyi points out that the best way to proceed would be to gather as many helpers as possible and set to work freely on the puzzle. Each individual would work on a specific element, but always keep an eye on what the other people are doing in order to learn from their mistakes and successes (LL, 43). Clearly, though, this would be an effective means to solving the puzzle only if all the participants believed that the various pieces really added up to a coherent whole. In Polanyi's words,

> the coherence of science must be regarded as an expression of the common rootedness of scientists in the same spiritual reality. Then only can we properly understand that at every step,

each is pursuing a common underlying purpose and that each
can sufficiently judge—in general accordance with other scientific opinion—whether his contribution is valid or not. Only
then are the conditions for the spontaneous co-ordination of
scientists properly established (LL, 48).

A commitment to a common "spiritual reality" is what preserves
the second kind of freedom from descending into totalitarianism.
For, "if the spontaneous growth of scholarship requires that
scholars be dedicated to the service of a transcendent reality, then
this implies that they must be free from all temporal authority" (LL,
49). By temporal authority, of course, Polanyi is referring to the
authority of the state and not to the supervision of scientists by
scientists.

We see here a union of the two kinds of freedom. Both are
necessary to the practice of science, but they rest on resources
that the other provides: individual freedom is restrained by an
authority that is created by the practitioners themselves, but is
ultimately rooted in a common commitment to transcendent
ideals; the second kind of freedom must always include the
individual exercise of conscience in the service of ends to which
all are committed.

Of course, the rules of science are not set in stone; alterations
may be introduced in the very act of scientific practice. As Polanyi
states, "all standards of professional success undergo some change
in the course of professional practice, and on the other hand even
the most daring pioneer in science accepts the general conception
of scientific achievement and bases his scientific claims essentially

on traditional standards" (LL, 61). This important truth was famously pointed out by T. S. Eliot in his essay, "Tradition and the Individual Talent."[27] For Eliot, innovation in poetry always and necessarily occurs in the context of tradition. In a 1962 essay dealing with originality in science, Polanyi quotes this passage from Eliot:

> We dwell with satisfaction upon the poet's difference from his predecessors, especially his immediate predecessors; we endeavour to find something that can be isolated in order to be enjoyed. Whereas if we approach a poet without this prejudice, we shall often find that not only the best, but the most individual parts of his work may be those in which the dead poets, his ancestors, assert their immortality most vigorously (quoted in KB, 67).

The poet and the scientist, Polanyi suggests, are in similar situations. The innovator has, as it were, one foot firmly rooted in the past with the masters who have preceded him, for even the most radical rebel or innovator must have an orthodoxy against which to rebel. His creative act must always occur in the context of the tradition of which he is a part. Eliot himself recognized the affinity between his own understanding of creativity and Polanyi's. In a 1945 letter, Eliot wrote: "It seems to me that your more exact examination of the nature of scientific enquiry and its relation to Government, confirms the sort of conclusions I have been for some time coming to about the nature of art (especially of course literature) and its relation to Government."[28]

The scientist and poet, then, face quite the same situation. Both find themselves yoked to the twin demands of authority and freedom. And this union of authority and freedom helps us to see how both aspects of freedom are necessary for the practice of science:

> Science, we can see now, shows strong features corresponding to both aspects of freedom. The assertion of his personal passion is the mark of the great pioneer, who is the salt of the earth in science. Originality is the principle virtue of a scientist and the revolutionary character of scientific progress is indeed proverbial. At the same time science has a most closely knit professional tradition; it rivals the Church of Rome and the legal profession in continuity of doctrine and strength of corporate spirit. Scientific rigour is as proverbial as scientific radicalism. Science fosters a maximum of originality while imposing also an exceptional degree of critical rigour (LL, 48).

Politics

When a rigorous fidelity to science is coupled with a materialistic conception of reality, the implications can extend far beyond the realm of science: the very core of moral and political structures can unravel. Harry Prosch, who coauthored Polanyi's last book, *Meaning*, notes that Polanyi's "critique of contemporary epistemology was, in fact, generated by an ethical problem: the damage he thought this epistemology was doing to our moral ideals."[29] Indeed, the moral and political implications of objectivism are a frequent topic in Polanyi's writings. This is perhaps not surprising given Polanyi's firsthand experience with political oppression and his lifelong concern about the philosophical roots of totalitarianism. Polanyi's account of the moral and political implications of objectivism begins with an account of the historic changes wrought by modern philosophy.

As we have seen, the scientific revolution led by such men as Descartes and Bacon included a disdain for any knowledge based on tradition or authority.[30] At a certain level this rejection was warranted, for in the limited range of scientific investigation, empirical observation must be given a prominent role. The success of science in the last three centuries attests to the positive impact of a rejection of certain assumptions that find their roots in Aristotelian metaphysics and sanctioned interpretations of biblical texts. But while a limited rejection of tradition and authority benefited the scientific enterprise, the momentum of modern philosophy continued to push toward a wholesale rejection of all tradition and authority—including social tradition and political authority. This trend culminated in the intellectual and political events surrounding the French Revolution. In light of the radical shift in orientation away from tradition and authority, Polanyi argues that history can be divided into two periods. All societies that preceded the revolution in France "accepted existing customs and law as the foundations of society." Although there "had been changes and some great reforms . . . never had the deliberate contriving of unlimited social improvement been elevated to a dominant principle" (SEP, 79).[31] By contrast to prior static societies, the French revolutionaries embraced with zeal the ideal of the unlimited progress of man both morally and materially. "[T]he end of the eighteenth century marks the dividing line between the immense expanse of essentially static societies and the brief period during which public life has become increasingly dominated by fervent expectations of a better future" (SEP, 79).

This optimistic and passionate drive toward human perfection was accompanied by an objectivist view of knowledge. As we have seen, the combination of Cartesian doubt and Lockean empiricism produced a view of reality that precluded any truth claims not admitting of empirical justification. Religious and moral claims were *a priori* ruled out of bounds. The authority of religion, specifically of Christianity—which had held a dominant position for nearly eighteen centuries—was undercut at its foundations. Scientism became the new religion. Its priests, the scientists and modern philosophers, used epistemological objectivism as their instrument of worship.

Skepticism, of course, was not unprecedented: it was a guiding principle of the ancient Stoics. Modern skepticism is different, however, because it occurs in a culture steeped in the residue of Christianity. "The ever-unquenching hunger and thirst after righteousness which our civilization carries in its blood as a heritage of Christianity does not allow us to settle down in the Stoic manner of antiquity" (M, 20). Thus, although objectivism does not permit consideration of the truth claims of Christianity, the memory of Christianity remains. This memory produces a passionate urge to pursue righteousness, even though objectivism has denied the very reality of moral truth. Polanyi describes this situation as follows:

> In such men the traditional forms for holding moral ideals had been shattered and their moral passions diverted into the only channels which a strictly mechanistic conception of man and

society left open to them. We may describe this as a process of *moral inversion*. The morally inverted person has not merely performed a philosophical substitution of material purposes for moral aims; he is acting with the whole force of his homeless moral passions within a purely materialistic framework of purposes (M, 18).

Moral inversion, then, consists in a combination of skeptical rationalism and moral perfectionism, which is nothing more than the "secularized fervour of Christianity" (KB, 10).[32] But whereas moral perfectionism within a Christian context is moderated by the doctrine of original sin and the deferral of perfection to the end of history, the perfectionism of a post-Christian world provides no such moderating counterbalances. The passionate perfectionism of Christianity remains despite a rejection of the doctrines that formerly prevented it from wreaking havoc on the society committed to its ideal. Furthermore, skeptical rationalism prevents any justification of Western man's moral impulses. This seemingly contradictory marriage of incompatible elements allows individuals and societies to commit appallingly immoral acts—acts which, according to the skeptic, are not really immoral since morality is an empty category. And such acts are committed in the name of perfectionism—a longing rooted in Christian doctrines that are no longer believable.

Thus, the ideal of moral perfection, which in Christianity was rooted in the transcendent, was immantentized or materialized by objectivism. This immanentization allowed scientific methods to be brought to bear on what were heretofore moral and religious affairs. Science now sanctioned impulses previously seen as immoral in an attempt to bring about a purely immanent perfection without the hindrance of moral limitations on the means to that end. But why, Polanyi asks, should such an obviously contradictory doctrine be held—especially by moderns, who pride themselves on their intellectual rigor? "The answer is, I believe, that it enables the modern mind, tortured by moral self-doubt, to indulge its moral passions in terms which also satisfy its passion for ruthless objectivity" (PK, 228).

Polanyi distinguishes between two manifestations of this combination of skepticism and moral perfectionism. The first is personal, while the second is political. The first is found in the modern nihilist: if traditional morality has no justification, man's choice is all that exists apart from the bare facts of science. All moral ideals are thus discredited. "We have, then, moral passions filled with contempt for their own ideals. And once they shun their own ideals, moral passions can express themselves only in anti-moralism" (TD, 58). The nihilist denies any distinction between good and evil. Thus, on the personal level, moral inversion produces the individual nihilist—Turgenev's Bazarov or Dostoyevsky's Raskolnikov, for example. The second manifestation is political. When skepticism and moral perfectionism are embraced, the political restraints provided by traditional morality are destroyed. The perfectionist element demands "the total transformation of society" (TD, 59). But because moral distinctions are denied, no limits are imposed on the political means used to achieve the desired result (TD, 58). In political terms, therefore, moral inversion produces the political excesses described by Dostoyevsky in *The Possessed* or, more generally, those of twentieth-century totalitarianism.

Yet here we encounter a curious puzzle: how is it that some modern societies apparently escaped the frenzied passion produced by moral inversion while others did not? This question is important, because it appears that all modern Western societies have, in large part, embraced the twin elements that constitute moral inversion: namely skepticism and moral perfectionism. The answer, according to Polanyi, is what he terms "pseudo-substitution." In short, those societies that avoided the descent into the abyss of political excess in fact continued to embrace traditional morality in practice even as they denied its reality in theory. "Men may go on talking the language of positivism, pragmatism, and naturalism for many years, yet continue to respect the principles of truth and morality which their vocabulary anxiously ignores" (PK, 233). Polanyi argues that both Britain and America have managed to escape the grim inhumanity of moral inversion by virtue of this dichotomy between practice and theory. This achievement was rendered possible by a sort of "suspended logic," one which allowed the British and Americans to avoid pursuing their theoretical positions to their practical conclusions (KB, 22).[33]

While this solution enables one to avoid the negative consequences of moral inversion, it is less than ideal. Far from dispensing with the problem, it only holds it at bay through self-trickery. Eventually, a more suitable solution must be found. The problem of moral inversion is, for Polanyi, the direct result of objectivism, which does not acknowledge moral truth as legitimate. While it is true that modern man has, due to his partial rejection of tradition and authority, produced innumerable technological advances, the pendulum has swung too far in the direction of rationalism and skepticism. Thus, modern man "must restore the balance between his critical powers and his moral demands" (SEP, 105). This restoration, as we will see, must take the form of a turn in the direction of the Augustinian tradition, for St. Augustine, like Polanyi, recognized the fiduciary element undergirding all rational thought.

What Polanyi refers to as a recovery of balance between man's moral demands and his critical powers indicates a more stable solution to the problem of moral inversion, for it attempts to overcome the epistemological shortcomings of modernity. These shortcomings created the possibility of moral inversion in the first place. A recognition of what Polanyi calls the "a-critical framework" of our knowledge would re-open the possibility of authoritative moral truth. The ensuing moral recovery would destroy skepticism and thereby knock out one of the legs supporting moral inversion. Furthermore, such a recovery would once again make possible legitimate religious discourse, thereby opening the door to a more suitable, religiously informed anthropology. Such an anthropology, in turn, would knock out moral inversion's second leg by tempering perfectionism. A return to orthodox Christianity is perhaps unlikely, but it is not, in Polanyi's argument, a necessary condition for avoiding the perils of moral inversion. A return to traditional religious forms might, however, be one of the outcomes produced by overcoming the prevailing objectivist epistemology in favor of a theory of knowledge that recognizes the fiduciary framework upon which all knowing rests.

CHAPTER THREE

THE TACIT DIMENSION: A NEW PARADIGM FOR KNOWING

IN THE PREFACE TO HIS 1951 collection of essays titled *The Logic of Liberty,* Polanyi notes that the book represents "my consistently renewed efforts to clarify the position of liberty in response to a number of questions raised by our troubled period of history." The essays deal with various aspects of liberty in relation to scientific, economic, and social concerns, and, Polanyi affirms, they have "evoked some valid answers, proved in battle." But he recognizes that a fully adequate account will have to go deeper. "I have thought of melting down the material and casting it into a mould of a comprehensive system, but this seemed premature. It cannot be attempted without establishing first a better foundation than we possess today for the holding of our beliefs (LL, xvii).

At the time he wrote the preface to *The Logic of Liberty,* Polanyi was busy preparing his Gifford Lectures (later published as *Personal Knowledge*). This project sought to provide the theoretical foundation for belief, which he recognized to be a necessary condition for a fully coherent defense of liberty. The theory of tacit knowing articulated in the Gifford Lectures, and refined and extended for the rest of his career, represents the heart of Polanyi's accomplishment as a philosopher.

A Return to St. Augustine

As we have seen, modern philosophy is characterized by a concerted rejection of tradition. In its stead rose the view Polanyi called "objectivism," a view embracing a completely detached ideal of knowledge. Polanyi recognized that all knowledge is dependent. The Cartesian ideal of achieving a God's-eye view (what Descartes called an Archimedean Point) from which to survey all objects of knowledge independently of any prior assumptions is an impossible (and ultimately harmful) dream. If that is the case, then the objectivist ideal must be overcome. In Polanyi's phrase, a "post-critical philosophy" must be developed.

Polanyi first situates his theory using broad historical brushstrokes. Philosophy was born in Greece, and Greek rationalism reigned until the spiritual fervor of Christianity reached a climax with the thought of St. Augustine. In the intellectual struggle leading up to his conversion, Augustine, who had once expressed a great admiration for and interest in science, came to consider "all scientific knowledge as barren and its pursuit as spiritually misleading" (SFS, 26). This sentiment solidified after his conversion, and his teaching on the matter "destroyed interest in science all over Europe for a thousand years" (PK, 141). According to Polanyi, Augustine "brought the history of Greek philosophy to a close by inaugurating for the first time a post-critical philosophy. He taught that all knowledge was a gift of grace, for which we must strive under the guidance of antecedent belief: *nisi credideritis, non intelligetis*" (PK, 266).[1] For the ancient Greeks, reason was primary. Augustine overturned that tradition by arguing that faith preceded reason. Modern philosophy, in turn, rejected the Augustinian primacy of belief with its rejection of all forms of tradition. Polanyi's critique of modern thought reveals its incoherencies. Modern thought has reached a dead end, and in order to remedy the error, Polanyi claims, "we must now go back to St. Augustine to restore the balance of our cognitive powers" (PK, 266).[2] In other words, we need a new, postcritical philosophy.

Polanyi is quick to point out that he does not repudiate the incredible gains made in the modern period, especially in the twin realms of science and technology. "Ever since the French Revolution, and up to our own days, scientific rationalism has been a major influence toward intellectual, moral, and social progress" (TD, 57). Yet, this obvious progress had a dark side. Writing as a European Jew, Polanyi was all too aware that the achievements of modern rationalism could be employed in support of terrifying ends. The dream of inevitable progress inspired by the ubiquity of modern rationalism was hollow. While he is loathe to dismiss the real material gains of modernity, Polanyi is also convinced that the moral and political tragedies of the twentieth century have revealed the logical consequences of modern rationalism. "The question is: Can we get rid of all these malignant excrescences of the scientific outlook without jettisoning the benefits which it can still yield to us both mentally and materially?" (M, 28). Ultimately, the problem must be dealt with at its roots: a new approach to knowledge must be proposed.

Keeping these awful aspects of our situation tacitly in mind, I shall try to trace a new line of thought along which, I believe, we may recover some of the ground rashly abandoned by the modern scientific outlook. I believe indeed, that this kind of effort, if pursued systematically, may eventually restore the balance between belief and reason on lines essentially similar to those marked out by Augustine at the dawn of Christian rationalism (FR, 238–39).[3]

Notice here and elsewhere that Polanyi employs the phrase "restore the balance" when referring to his post-critical philosophy. The notion of balance is an important one. The historical progression that he describes elicits the picture of a pendulum. Greek rationalism represents the pendulum at one extreme. It was rejected by Augustine, whose ideas forced the pendulum far in the opposite direction. Modern rationalism, in turn, rejected Augustine and returned the pendulum hard in the direction of rationalism. The idea of balance, on the other hand, implies a proper relationship between reason and belief. Polanyi's call for a return to Augustine is not a call to reject all appeals to reason or to deny the importance of science or other secular pursuits; instead, it is a call to recognize the indispensable role belief plays in all knowing.

We must now recognize belief once more as the source of all knowledge. Tacit assent and intellectual passions, the sharing of an idiom and of a cultural heritage, affiliation to a like-minded community: such are the impulses which shape our vision of the nature of things on which we rely for our mastery of things.

THE TACIT DIMENSION   63

No intelligence, however critical or original, can operate outside such a fiduciary framework (PK, 266).

This fiduciary framework can exist only in a social context rooted
in a particular tradition into which members are inculcated.

Tradition and Authority

Knowing is an art, and any art is learned by apprenticeship and
practice. Therefore, the mere learning of rules is not the primary
manner by which an art is acquired. "Rules of art can be useful, but
they do not determine the practice of an art; they are maxims, which
can serve as a guide to an art only if they can be integrated into the
practical knowledge of the art. They cannot replace this knowledge" (PK, 50).[4] This emphasis on practical knowledge directly
contradicts the modern prejudice in favor of explicitness. Francis
Bacon, for example, insisted that, if only his inductive method were
applied, all people would "fall into our way of interpretation
without the aid of any art."[5] Polanyi, on the other hand, understood
that practical knowledge precedes the knowledge of rules, for one
must possess a degree of practical knowledge in order properly to
apply rules. One acquires practical knowledge through doing. But
how can one practice an art if one does not yet know how to do so?
The answer lies in submission to an authority in the manner of an
apprentice. We learn by example:

> To learn by example is to submit to authority. You follow your
> master because you trust his manner of doing things even when

you cannot analyse and account in detail for its effectiveness. By watching the master and emulating his efforts in the presence of his example, the apprentice unconsciously picks up the rules of the art, including those which are not explicitly known to the master himself. These hidden rules can be assimilated only by a person who surrenders himself to that extent uncritically to the imitation of another (PK, 53).[6]

In learning by submitting to the authority of a teacher, the pupil seeks to grasp what he initially does not comprehend. In other words, the student must attempt to dwell in a practice he does not yet understand. "In order to share this indwelling, the pupil must presume that a teaching which appears meaningless to start with has in fact a meaning which can be discovered by hitting on the same kind of indwelling as the teacher is practicing. Such an effort is based on accepting the teacher's authority" (TD, 61).

But if knowing is an art, and if learning an art requires dwelling in the practices of a master, then it follows that there must exist a tradition by which an art is transmitted. Furthermore, any attempts categorically and systematically to reject tradition must be logically incompatible with knowing. If this is the case, then we must conclude that the ideal of tradition-free inquiry is simply impossible. "No human mind can function without accepting authority, custom, and tradition: it must rely on them for the mere use of a language" (KB, 41). Indeed, according to Polanyi, "all human thought comes into existence by grasping the meaning and mastering the use of language," (KB, 160). To the extent that language is required for thought, tradition and authority are necessary for knowing even in the earliest developmental stages. A child, for example, must put his trust in the language-speakers around him and seek to dwell in the particulars of the language before he can master it. He does not begin by learning rules of grammar and syntax, for the rules themselves require language in order to be formulated. In the same way, any skill must first be acquired through submission to the authority of a particular tradition. The skill itself exists primarily in its practice and only secondarily in rules, which are necessarily formulated subsequent to the practice. Tradition, it seems, plays an indispensable role in the knowledge that we acquire; thus,

> it appears that traditionalism, which requires us to believe before we know, and in order that we may know, is based on a deeper insight into the nature of knowledge and of the communication of knowledge than is a scientific rationalism that would permit us to believe only explicit statements based on tangible data and derived from these by a formal inference, open to repeated testing (TD, 61–62).

Polanyi, whose epistemological concerns are at least partially motivated by political and moral concerns, employs a political example to make his point. Polanyi construes the modern political scene as a confrontation between the followers of Edmund Burke and the followers of Thomas Paine. Burke, of course, denounced the French Revolution as a dangerous and destructive event, for its leaders sought to overturn all traditional practices and values and to construct *ex nihilo* a new and better society dedicated to serving the rights of man and engaging in practices derived from rational thought alone. Paine, on the other hand, embraced the ideals of the French Revolution and argued that each society ought to be free to begin anew, just as the French did. Polanyi recognized that many of his modern contemporaries embraced the ideals of Paine and eschewed the traditionalism of Burke. But, he argued, that embrace is ambivalent, for although in theory most moderns advocate the radical liberty of Paine, in practice many—especially the British and the Americans—are Burkeans. "In actual practice it is Burke's vision that controls the British nation; the voice is Esau's, but the hand is Jacob's" (KB, 68). Polanyi argued that Britain has enjoyed political stability because the British generally "profess the right of absolute self-determination in *political theory* and [rely] on the guidance of tradition in *political practice*" (KB, 68). He therefore advocates a dynamic blend of Paine's progressivism and Burke's traditionalism:

> I will not resist in any way the momentum of the French Revolution. I accept its dynamism. But I believe that the new self-determination of man can be saved from destroying itself only by recognizing its own limits in an authoritative traditional framework which upholds it. Tom Paine could proclaim the right of each generation to determine its institutions anew, since the range of his demands was in fact very modest. He unquestioningly accepted the continuity of culture and of the order of private property as the framework of self-determination. Today the ideas of Tom Paine can be saved from self-destruction only by a conscious reaffirmation of traditional continuity. Paine's ideal of unlimited gradual progress can be saved from destruction by revolution only by the kind of traditionalism taught by Paine's opponent, Edmund Burke (TD, 62–63).

Thus, the traditionalism that Polanyi advocates is in no way static. Polanyi's high appreciation for scientific discovery leads him to comprehend tradition as an orthodoxy that enforces a kind of discipline on those subject to the tradition; but the orthodoxy is a dynamic one in that "it implicitly grants the right to opposition in the name of truth" (KB, 70). According to Polanyi, this view of tradition

> transcends the conflict between Edmund Burke and Tom Paine. It rejects Paine's demand for the absolute self-determination of each generation, but does so for the sake of its own ideal of unlimited human and social improvement. It accepts Burke's thesis that freedom must be rooted in tradition, but transposes it into a system cultivating radical progress (KB, 71).

As this description of tradition indicates, while Polanyi embraces an Augustinian approach to epistemology, he is decidedly non-Augustinian in his view of social progress. On the one hand, his epistemological position results from his recognition that modern critical philosophy is ultimately unsustainable, and that "the balance of our cognitive powers" can only be restored by forcing the pendulum back toward Augustine. But on the other hand, the obvious advances that were made in the modern era were at least in part due to modern philosophy having loosed itself from the constraints of the past. Such advances make him much more optimistic about the prospects for social progress than was Augustine.

Furthermore, tradition, for Polanyi, is not a simple and stable resource that can be accessed in a purely objective fashion. Polanyi's traditionalism is dynamic in that it encourages a degree of dissent. But it is more fundamentally dynamic in that we cannot participate in a tradition without changing it. "Traditions are transmitted to us from the past, but they are our own interpretations of the past, at which we have arrived within the context of our own immediate problems" (PK, 160). Thus, each generation appropriates a tradition, but the appropriation necessarily entails interpretation. Interpretation, in turn, is necessarily conducted in light of the concerns, biases, and circumstances of the particular generation appropriating the tradition. In addition, each person who participates in a tradition contributes to the further development of the tradition.

Community

A tradition, of course, requires the presence of a community committed to its perpetuation. Since knowing is an art that requires one to enter into its practice through submission to the authority of a master, and since traditions are embodied in and transmitted through practices, knowing is fundamentally social. That is, traditions do not exist apart from the communities that embrace them and transmit them to subsequent generations. Thus, knowledge is not merely social; it is communal, for traditions persist only in communities that embrace, whether tacitly or explicitly, a particular tradition as an orthodoxy.

If knowing is rooted in submission to tradition and authority, it follows that belief precedes knowing—even in the practice of science. Belief, of course, cannot exist except within a community.

As we have seen, even language requires belief. When a child learns a language, he believes (trusts) that the language-speakers who surround him are not uttering gibberish.Likewise, all skills require submission to a master because the novice does not yet comprehend what he is practicing. Science is no different, for the aspiring scientist must submit himself to the authority of a practicing scientist, and such submission requires belief. "Thus," in Polanyi's words, "to accord validity to science—or to any other of the great domains of the mind—is to express a faith which can be upheld only within a community. We realize here the connexion between Science, Faith and Society" (SFS, 73).[7] Thus, knowing requires the existence of a society committed to a particular tradition and engaged in passing it on. This is not to say that knowledge is only possible within a homogeneous community. Indeed, a particular society may be comprised of various competing traditions. But the social nature of knowing depends on the existence of social structures, each grounded in a particular tradition or set of traditions.

Of course, the adherents of a tradition are often not explicitly aware of that to which they are committed; often the premises of a tradition "lie deeply embedded in the unconscious foundations of practice" (SFS, 76). These premises are tacitly passed on to the next generation through education in the practices by which the tradition is constituted. Knowing, then, is in its essence, communal:

> Articulate systems which foster and satisfy an intellectual passion
> can survive only with the support of a society which respects the
> values affirmed by these passions, and a society has a cultural life
> only to the extent to which it acknowledges and fulfils the obliga-

tion to lend its support to the cultivation of these passions. Since the advancement and dissemination of knowledge by the pursuit of science, or technology and mathematics forms part of cultural life, the tacit coefficients by which these articulate systems are understood and accredited, and which uphold quite generally our shaping and affirmation of factual truth, are also coefficients of a cultural life shared by a community (PK, 203).

Tacit Knowing

The fiduciary element of knowing extends to a more fundamental level even than the acquisition of language. Polanyi's most significant insight concerns the basic operation of the mind: all knowing consists of the integration of subsidiary and tacitly sensed particulars into a focal and articulate whole. Polanyi draws upon the insights of Gestalt psychology to make his point.

How do we recognize a face? This is an apparently simple question, but it is actually quite complex. Humans can easily pick out one face—a friend, a spouse, or an acquaintance—from a line-up of a hundred or a million. But if we asked for a description of the process, the person who so readily identified the face would be hard pressed to explain *how* he knew. In other words, it appears that "we can know more than we can tell" (TD, 4). Of course, all faces are different, and the particular features of each—the shape of the nose, the size of the mouth, the spatial relationship of eyes to mouth, the curve of cheek and lines of the chin—all combine to form the particular physiognomy that we recognize instantly.

Gestalt psychology, in Polanyi's words, claims that "the particulars of a pattern or a tune must be apprehended jointly, for if you observe the particulars separately they form no pattern or tune" (PK, 56–57).[8] In terms of the present example, Polanyi writes that "Gestalt psychology has demonstrated that we may know a physiognomy by integrating our awareness of its particulars without being able to identify these particulars" (TD, 6). But while Gestalt psychologists understand this integration as a passive event, Polanyi disagrees: "I am looking at Gestalt, on the contrary, as the outcome of an active shaping of experience performed in the pursuit of knowledge. This shaping or integrating I hold to be the great and indispensable tacit power by which all knowledge is discovered and, once discovered, is held to be true" (TD, 6).[9] From this it becomes clear that, for Polanyi, all knowledge "is either tacit or rooted in tacit knowledge" (KB, 195). This insight represents the heart of Polanyi's theory of knowledge.

Knowing, according to Polanyi, comprises two types of awareness: the subsidiary and the focal. Focal awareness concerns the conscious object of our attention. But all focal awareness is dependent on subsidiary awareness. We attend focally to the object of our attention while dwelling subsidiarily in a variety of clues that stand in the background and make attending to the focal target possible. The integration of these two kinds of awareness occurs in any act of knowing. Polanyi gives his readers several examples that clarify this distinction.

1) As we have already seen, the particulars of a physiognomy are not immediately specifiable, yet a familiar person is recognized without hesitation. The particular features of the physiognomy are

subsidiarily known and the integration of the particulars produces the recognizable face, which is the focus of our attention. In other words, we do not focus upon any particular facial feature; instead, we focus upon the face as a whole. The joint relationship between the subsidiaries and the focal produce a recognizable countenance (TD, 46; KB, 123).

2) A stereoscope is an instrument in which two pictures of the same object are observed, each by one eye. The pictures are taken from slightly different angles. The image produced by the tacit integration of the two pictures yields a three-dimensional depth that neither of the single pictures possesses. In this case, we attend subsidiarily to the two pictures and focus on their integration. The integration, of course, will be destroyed if our focus is shifted to the particular pictures (LP, 29).

3) When a person employs a probe to explore a hidden cavity, or when a blind person uses a stick to find his way along an unknown path, the individual is aware of the impact the handle produces on his hand when the probe strikes an object, but he attends to these impacts subsidiarily. His focus is upon the end of the stick. By attending focally to that while attending subsidiarily to the impact of the stick on his hand, he is able to comprehend objects beyond the stick. In a certain respect, the probe becomes an extension of his own body. For this reason, subsidiary awareness and focal awareness can be understood in terms of physiology and identified as proximal and distal. The proximal term is closest to one's body—in effect, it is either part of one's body (as with a hand or limb), or becomes an extension of one's body (as with a probe or any other tool). We dwell subsidiarily in the proximal term in order

to focus upon the distal term (PK, 55–56; KB, 127–28).¹⁰ Thus, the subsidiary-focal relationship can be characterized as a *from-to* relation. We attend *from* the subsidiaries *to* the focal target.

4) A skillful performance requires the same tacit integration of subsidiary and focal elements. For example, if a piano player shifts the focus of his attention from the piece he is playing to the particular movement of his fingers, he will very likely become confused and have to stop. In the same way, an athlete will be unable to specify all that goes into a skillful performance of his particular sport. If he is asked to identify each component explicitly, he will be unable to comply; and if, while performing, he turns his focus on the particulars of that performance, his performance will likely fail (PK, 56; KB, 125–26). Thus, "subsidiary awareness and focal awareness are mutually exclusive" (PK, 56). Furthermore, "focal and subsidiary awareness are definitely *not two degrees* of attention but *two kinds* of attention given to the *same* particulars" (KB, 128).

5) When we use language, the dual structure of subsidiary and focal awareness again becomes evident. When we read words, we attend focally to the meaning of the words as we attend subsidiarily to the words and the letters by which they are constituted. If we turn our focus to the words themselves, we lose their meaning. For example, if we repeat a particular word over and over, the word soon becomes meaningless noise. Once we return our focus to the meaning of the word and attend only subsidiarily to the word itself, integration is restored; the word once again functions as a carrier of meaning. In a certain respect, we look *through* the word to its meaning. When we shift our attention to the word itself, when we no longer look through it but *at* it, the tacit integration is

lost and the word becomes a meaningless symbol (PK, 57).[11] Polanyi illustrates this point using a personal anecdote:

> My correspondence arrives at my breakfast table in various languages, but my son understands only English. Having just finished reading a letter I may wish to pass it on to him, but must check myself and look again to see in what language it was written. I am vividly aware of the meaning conveyed by the letter, yet know nothing whatever of its words. I have attended to them closely but only for what they mean and not for what they are as objects. If my understanding of the text were halting, or its expressions or its spelling were faulty, its words would arrest my attention. They would become slightly opaque and prevent my thought from passing through them unhindered to the things they signify (PK, 57).

It is important to recognize, though, that subsidiary awareness is not unconscious awareness. Instead,

> the level of consciousness at which we are aware of a subsidiary particular may vary over the whole range of possible levels. Some subsidiary things, like the processes in our inner ear, of which we are aware in feeling the position of our head, are profoundly unconscious, strictly subliminal. But we are not unconscious of a pointing finger the direction of which we are following, nor of the features of a face that we are seeking to recognize, nor of the paper and pen used with a bearing on the content of a written message we are composing (KB, 197).

Polanyi identifies four aspects of tacit knowing. Each reveals

one way in which the tacit integration of particulars produces more than the mere sum of disparate parts. First, the from-to aspect of tacit knowing—the element by which we attend subsidiarily to certain things while attending focally to the object of our attention—can be called the *functional* structure of tacit knowing. Second, the integration of subsidiary and focal objects changes the appearance of what we know. Take, for example, the stereoscope. The tacit integration produces a three-dimensional image. In Polanyi's words, "we are aware of the proximal term of an act of tacit knowing in the appearance of its distal term; we are aware of that *from* which we are attending *to* another thing, in the *appearance* of that thing" (TD, 11). This change in appearance can be termed the *phenomenal* structure of tacit knowing. Next, when the integration of subsidiaries and the focal elements occurs, new meaning emerges. This new meaning was not available prior to the act of tacit integration. For example, when we employ a probe to explore the interior of a cavity, we attend subsidiarily to the impact of the tool on our hands as we focus on the meaning derived from the distal end of the probe. In Polanyi's words, "we are attending to the meaning of its impact on our hands in terms of its effect on the things to which we are applying it" (TD, 13). This new meaning that emerges in the wake of the integration is the *semantic* aspect of tacit knowing. Finally, the functional, phenomenal, and semantic aspects of tacit knowing combine to reveal something that does not simply appear different or mean more, but actually is more than the sum of the particulars themselves. "The transposition of bodily experiences into the perception of things outside may now appear, therefore, as an instance of the transposition of meaning away from us, which we have found to be present to some extent in all tacit knowing" (TD, 14). The recognition of an entity independent of and external to us is what Polanyi understands as the fourth aspect of tacit knowing: its *ontological* aspect.

The from-to nature of tacit knowing reveals some important features of the tacit dimension of human cognition. First, it puts the human knower at the center of the knowing process. This is the central motivating purpose of Polanyi's epistemological project. He seeks to refute the modern ideal of strict detachment in which complete objectivity is achieved by removing the knower from the equation. In *Personal Knowledge,* Polanyi admits that the ideal of detachment is perhaps a harmless (though false) ideal when dealing with the exact sciences. But "it exercises a destructive influence in biology, psychology and sociology, and falsifies our whole outlook far beyond the domain of science. I want to establish an alternative ideal of knowledge, quite generally" (PK, vii).

As we have seen, the tacit dimension of knowing consists in an integration of two mutually exclusive elements—the subsidiary and the focal. In spatial terms, these are proximal and distal elements. In order to focus on any object, one must dwell in the subsidiaries while attending to the focal target. What we hold subsidiarily is the proximal term of the tacit relationship. It represents an extension of our bodies in the process of achieving a meaningful integration with the distal element. Because the proximal component of tacit knowing is rooted in our bodies and extends out from them, all thought is rooted in the body. That said, we are generally aware of our bodies only subsidiarily, and those things we employ subsidiarily while attending to the focal targets of our attention are in effect extensions of our bodies. Thus, "our body is the ultimate instrument of all our external knowledge, whether intellectual or practical" (TD, 15).[12] Indwelling, then, indicates the extension of the body in the process of knowing. Polanyi writes:

> The use of the term "indwelling" applies here in a logical sense as affirming that the parts of the external world that we interiorise function in the same way as our body functions when we attend from it to things outside. In this sense we live also in the tools and probes which we use, and likewise in our intellectual tools and probes. To apply a theory for understanding nature is to interiorise it. We attend *from* the theory *to* things interpreted in its light (SR, 8).

For Polanyi, then, the ideal of a strictly explicit knowledge is self-contradictory: "deprived of their tacit coefficients, all spoken words, all formulae, all maps and graphs, are strictly meaningless" (KB, 195).[13] In the same way that purely explicit knowledge is denied, so too is strict detachment. Tacit knowing requires the constant integrating activity of the knower. If, as we have seen, all knowledge is either tacit or rooted in tacit knowledge, then "all tacit knowing requires the continued participation of the knower, and a measure of personal participation is intrinsic therefore to all knowledge" (KB, 152). It is through indwelling that we participate: "All knowing is personal knowing—participation through indwelling" (M, 44). By claiming that knowledge requires the active and continued participation of the knower, Polanyi separates himself radically from those who embrace the ideal of passive and detached rationalism. Furthermore, by claiming that the body plays a central role in knowing, he sets himself up against Cartesian dualism, which understands the body as a mere physical extension and the mind as related only incidentally to the body.

Polanyi describes tacit knowing as a triad consisting of three components, each performing a particular and essential function. First, there are the subsidiaries we employ in focusing upon the second element: the object of our attention. The knower is the third essential ingredient, for the individual integrates the subsidiary and the focal in the active process that constitutes tacit knowing. But this triad is not necessarily permanent. Because "the subsidiaries have a meaning to the knower which fills the center of his focal attention . . . the knower can dissolve the triad by merely looking differently at the subsidiaries" (LP, 31). The image of a triad provides a useful framework for comprehending the dynamics of tacit knowing:

> Suppose, then, that it is possible, at least in principle, to identify all the subsidiaries of a triad; however elusive that may be we would still face the fact that anything serving as a subsidiary ceases to do so when focal attention is directed on it. It turns into a different kind of thing, deprived of the meaning it had in the triad. Thus subsidiaries are—in this important sense—essentially unspecifiable. We must distinguish, then, between two types of the unspecifiability of subsidiaries. One type is due to the difficulty of tracing the subsidiaries, a condition that is widespread but not universal—and the other type is due to a sense deprivation which is logically necessary and in principle absolute (LP, 31).

In other words, none of the three elements of the triad can be removed without destroying the meaning created in their tacit integration.

If Polanyi's account of knowing is accurate, the ideal of objective detachment is untenable, for the active participation of the knower is indispensable. Furthermore, if all knowing comes about in this triadic fashion, which necessarily includes elements that are unspecifiable, then we can agree with Polanyi that all knowledge is either tacit or rooted in tacit knowledge. The ideal of a purely explicit knowledge—the cherished goal of objectivism—is ultimately rendered impossible.

Realism

Meno's paradox is A recurring subject in Polanyi's work. Describing a puzzle that is central to the problem of discovery of any sort, the paradox can be summarized as follows: When we seek understanding, we either know what we are seeking or not. If we know what we are looking for, we need look no further, for we already possess the understanding. On the other hand, if we do not know what we are looking for, how can we proceed? It is impossible to pursue what we do not know, and it is unnecessary to pursue what we already possess.[14] Plato offered his theory of recollection as a solution to the paradox, but it has not worn well. Polanyi believes his theory of knowledge provides a satisfactory answer. As he puts it,

> the *Meno* shows conclusively that if all knowledge is explicit, i.e., capable of being clearly stated, then we cannot know a prob-

lem or look for its solution. And the *Meno* also shows, therefore, that if problems nevertheless exist, and discoveries can be
made by solving them, we can know things, and important
things, that we cannot tell (TD, 22).

Borrowing from mathematician Henri Poincaré, Polanyi lists
four stages of discovery: preparation, incubation, illumination,
and verification (PK, 121).[15] Preparation represents the time spent
immersed in the details of a problem—the necessary though not
sufficient groundwork, for without adequate preparation, one is
incapable of either adequately formulating a problem or of recognizing likely avenues to pursue its solution. Incubation is the
period during which the mind works on a problem, often when
explicit attention is focused on other things. This period is largely
unspecifiable. The solution becomes clear in a moment of illumination. This is the moment we exclaim "Eureka!" The particulars of the problem we have been working on suddenly coalesce
into a solution. The move from incubation to illumination is
unformalizable; in Polanyi's words, there is a "logical gap" between the particulars of a problem and its solution. "'Illumination' is then the leap by which the logical gap is crossed. It is the
plunge by which we gain a foothold at another shore of reality"
(PK, 123). Verification comes last. This is the period spent attempting to confirm what one already knows. Recall the instance from
the first chapter illustrating this very point: when Polanyi presented his dissertation to his professors at the University of
Budapest, one of them noted that Polanyi's conclusion seemed
correct but his mathematical derivation faulty. Much to the

professor's consternation, the young Polanyi replied that one often reaches a correct conclusion, and only then subsequently seeks to demonstrate it. Polanyi was fond of pointing to such figures as Kepler and Einstein, who through a process that included much work, grasped—in a moment of illumination—a significant discovery, only to spend much subsequent time and effort attempting to verify what they knew to be true (PK, 9–15).[16]

But what guides this progression that climaxes in illumination? Polanyi explains: "We can pursue scientific discovery [and by analogy all discovery] without knowing what we are looking for, because the gradient of deepening coherence tells us where to start and which way to turn, and eventually brings us to the point where we may stop and claim a discovery" (CI, 116). Thus, "we should look at the known data, but not in themselves, rather as clues to the unknown; as pointers to it and parts of it. We should strive persistently to feel our way towards an understanding of the manner in which these known particulars hang together, both mutually and with the unknown" (PK, 127–28). The particulars combine to reveal a previously unknown reality. Sometimes this process is immediate and requires no period of incubation, as with the use of a stereoscope. At other times, tacit integration requires significant time and labor and may only be verified long after the discovery has been made (KB, 119).

Throughout the process, the knower is guided by a deepening sense of coherence. If this were not so, the scientist, for example, would be compelled to attempt every possible solution to a problem. But that is simply not the case, for, as we have seen, a good scientist is able to anticipate with some accuracy whether or not a possible solution is likely to be correct. Polanyi calls this power "intuition" or "foreknowledge."

> But there exists also a more intensely pointed knowledge of hidden coherence; the kind of foreknowledge we call a problem. And we know that the scientist produces problems, has hunches, and elated by these anticipations, pursues the quest that should fulfill these anticipations. This quest is guided throughout by feelings of a deepening coherence and these feelings have a fair chance of proving right. We may recognize here the powers of dynamic intuition (CI, 116).

Polanyi does not assign a quasi-mystical status to intuition and foreknowledge. Instead, he merely acknowledges the unformalizable element that accompanies discovery. Intuition, for Polanyi, "is a skill for guessing with a reasonable chance of guessing right; a skill guided by an innate sensibility to coherence, improved by schooling" (CI, 117). Because it is a skill, intuition is neither infallible nor reducible to rules; yet at the same time, a well developed sense of intuition tends to be right. Thus, a well-trained practitioner—whether a scientist, a politician, an ethicist, or an athlete—exhibits an ability to guess skillfully that the novice simply does not posses (KB, 118). Finally, "intuition works on a subsidiary level," which attests to its unspecifiability (CI, 121).

When we speak of an object of intuition, we imply the existence of a reality that can be known. One of Polanyi's favorite phrases in describing the process of discovery is "contact with reality." He speaks of "contact with a hidden reality" and "intimation of a hidden reality." Realism is central to his thought, and he regularly affirms his commitment to that philosophical position.[17] This view of reality as hidden but existent justifies his account of discovery: the intimation of an unknown yet knowable coherence explains how one can pursue an answer that is as yet unknown. It also justifies Polanyi's claim that we can know more than we can tell. He writes:

> We can account for this capacity of ours to know more than we can tell if we believe in the presence of an external reality with which we can establish contact. This I do. I declare myself committed to the belief in an external reality gradually accessible to knowing, and I regard all true understanding as an intimation of such a reality which, being real, may yet reveal itself to our deepened understanding in an indefinite range of unexpected manifestations (KB, 133).

This description of reality contains at least four important points, which recur throughout Polanyi's work. First, reality is external to the knower; the essence of reality is not dependent upon the mind of the knower. It exists even if it is not apprehended. Second, reality is knowable, though not exhaustively. Our minds are so constituted that they can contact a reality that is external to them. Third, contact is gradual. We continually attempt to extend or strengthen our contact with reality, but it is not a once-and-for-all event. Instead, it is an endeavor we share with those who have gone before and anticipate for those who will come after us. Finally, the real, as real, might manifest itself in "indefinite" and "unexpected" ways. Thus, "when we accept the discovery as true, we commit ourselves to a belief in all these as yet undisclosed, perhaps as yet unthinkable, consequences" (TD, 23).

A further aspect of reality is the relationship between tangibles and intangibles. Modern materialistic philosophy has created a bias toward the tangible. But "the belief that, since particulars are more tangible, their knowledge offers a true conception of things is fundamentally mistaken" (TD, 19). For Polanyi, intangibles are more real than tangibles. He writes:

> I shall say . . . that minds and problems possess a deeper reality than cobblestones, although cobblestones are admittedly more real in the sense of being *tangible*. And since I regard the significance of a thing as more important than its tangibility, I shall say that minds and problems are more real than cobblestones (TD, 33).

Physical particulars are more tangible than ideas, for example, but if we recall the various aspects of tacit knowing, particulars are integrated in the act of tacit knowing. Their integration produces a phenomenal change, which has semantic and ultimately ontological significance. In other words, when particulars are combined in an act of tacit integration, they become more than the sum of their respective parts. The resulting Gestalten, if integrated successfully, are entities more real than the particulars of which they are composed. Thus, the intangible meaning of a tacit integration is more real than the tangible particulars of which it is composed. Furthermore, tangible particulars do not admit of the same range of indefinite and unexpected manifestations as intangibles; thus, "the vagueness of something like the human mind is due to the vastness of its resources. . . . By my definition, this indeterminacy makes mind the more real, the more substantial" (KB, 151).

In one essay, Polanyi writes that we "gradually penetrate to things that are increasingly real, things which, being real, may yet manifest themselves on an indeterminate range of future occasions" (KB, 168). The image of gradually penetrating to what is more real suggests a vision of reality in which the core is most real, while the fringes, though real, are not as real as what is closer to the core. But there is a paradox at the center of this conception of reality, a paradox that Polanyi has no interest in resolving: the closer we approach the real, the more indeterminate and unexpected will be our findings. This indeterminateness is not due to an essential randomness at the heart of reality; instead, it points to the infinite richness of reality. This richness of the real produces unexpected manifestations. Because we are finite, we will never reach the core of reality, a reality that presents us with infinite possibilities. The process of knowing presents us with continual surprises. If the more real is capable of manifesting itself in indeterminate and unexpected ways, the knowing process is open-ended and contingent. Furthermore, because it is conducted by imperfect individuals working within particular traditions, knowing is both fallible and colored by personal experiences.

Our Embeddedness

As we have seen, modern critical philosophy was characterized by a desire to destroy the influence that tradition exercises on each knower. The religious doctrines, moral maxims, and authorities to which premodern people quite willingly submitted themselves were denigrated. Individuals were "urged to resist the pressure of this traditional indoctrination by pitting against it the principle of philosophic doubt" (PK, 269). Demand proof. Believe nothing that has not been explicitly proved. Rid your mind of traditional belief, which is mere opinion, and obtain certainty by grounding all inquiry in pure reason. The ideal for this approach to knowledge is a virgin mind, one untainted by any belief that has not been derived from reason alone. But such a mind is not easy to produce. In fact, if one succeeded in producing it, the result would be something less than a human mind.

> A virgin mind must be allowed to mature until the age at which it reaches its full natural powers of intelligence, but would have to be kept unshaped until then by any kind of education. It must be taught no language, for speech can be acquired only a-critically, and the practice of speech in one particular language carries with it the acceptance of the particular theory of the universe postulated by that language (PK, 295).

Polanyi concludes this reflection by stating what should be apparent: "An entirely untutored mind would . . . result in a state of imbecility" (PK, 295). Thus, in order to avoid the absurd consequences of a virgin mind, we must acknowledge that we all are embedded in various ways—in our languages, histories, personal abilities, and cultures.

Language is, according to Polanyi, what separates humans from animals (PK, 69ff).[18] In fact, "all human thought comes into existence by grasping the meaning and mastering the use of language" (KB, 160). As we have seen, language (and therefore thought) is essentially social. As Polanyi puts it, "Human thought grows only within language, and since language can exist only in a society, all thought is rooted in society" (SM, 60). But humans do not share a universal language. A language consists of a stable yet malleable assortment of words and structures by which the speaker engages his society and his world. When we employ a particular language, then, "all questions we can ask will have to be formulated in it and will thereby confirm the theory of the universe which is implied in the vocabulary and structure of the language" (SB, 221).[19] In other words, the language we indwell constitutes the framework through which we see the world. Thus, "our most deeply ingrained convictions are determined by the idiom in which we interpret our experience and in terms of which we erect our articulate systems" (PK, 287). The a-critical nature of language acquisition implies that "the practice of speech in one particular language carries with it the acceptance of the particular theory of the universe postulated by that language" (PK, 295). By virtue of the linguistic character of thought, all humans are necessarily embedded within a particular linguistic tradition that is accepted a-critically. This linguistic tradition constitutes the framework through which the world is viewed and consequently establishes the parameters of thought.[20]

Second, humans are embedded within a particular culture. As with language, we enter into a particular cultural framework when we are born. "Members admitted to a community at birth cannot be given a free choice of their premises; they have to be educated in some terms or other, without consultation of any preference of their own" (SFS, 72). We initially accept the habits, traditions, religious and moral practices, etc., of a particular culture in an a-critical fashion. Polanyi writes: "The whole universe of human sensibility—

of our intellectual, moral, artistic, religious ideas—is evoked . . . by dwelling within the framework of our cultural heritage" (SM, 39). One's culture is comprehended by indwelling, and as we have seen, indwelling implies submission and trust. As Polanyi puts it, "the sharing of an idiom and of a cultural heritage, affiliation to a like-minded community: such are the impulses which shape our vision of the nature of things on which we rely for our mastery of things. No intelligence, however critical or original, can operate outside such a fiduciary framework" (PK, 266).

Third, human thought is constituted in part by the historical setting in which it occurs. The objectivist believes that the individual can fully transcend his historical situation and grasp truth unmediated by the vicissitudes of his historical moment. But this is impossible. This point perhaps can be made clear if we remember that languages and cultures change and develop over time. That being the case, the particular historical time one inhabits will be framed by the particular language and culture into which one is inculcated. But if linguistic and cultural frameworks change with time, and if language and culture provide the framework through which we see and interpret the world, then in an important way *when* one lives serves to constitute in large part *how* one sees the world (PK, 171, 324).

If we are embedded, therefore, within a language, a culture, and a historical moment in such a way that the framework by which we comprehend the world is, in part, constituted by the language, culture, and historical moment in which we dwell, then it is foolishness to imagine the possibility of getting completely outside of that framework in order to critique it. The linguistic, cultural, and historical moment in which one dwells represents the particular tradition to which one belongs. This same tradition provides us with the tools by which to mount a critique. To imagine evaluating one's particular tradition from outside all traditions is tantamount to critiquing one's particular language by standing outside any language. It is self-contradictory. As Polanyi puts it, "I cannot speak except from inside a language" (PK, 253).

Finally—and this bears remembering—we are all limited by our personal capacities. Polanyi writes: "I must admit that I can fulfil my obligation to serve the truth only to the extent of my natural abilities as developed by my education. No one can transcend his formative milieu very far, and beyond this area he must rely on it uncritically" (KB, 133). Our individual capacities are fixed, although they can be extended or directed through education. "Although our fundamental propensities are innate, they are vastly modified and enlarged by our upbringing" (PK, 267). Not everyone is capable of genius, despite the best education. Furthermore, innate strengths in one area may be accompanied by weaknesses in others. In other words, all humans possess personal capacities which may be developed and directed but which cannot be exceeded.

Polanyi readily admits that his own thought is unavoidably colored by who he is. In other words, he admits that he does not attempt to begin his inquiry as a virgin mind or as a universal doubter, both of which are absurd ideals:

> I must admit now that I did not start the present reconsideration of my beliefs with a clean slate of unbelief. Far from it. I started as a person intellectually fashioned by a particular idiom, acquired through my affiliation to a civilization that prevailed

in the places where I had grown up, at this particular period of
history. This has been the matrix of all my intellectual efforts.
Within it I was to find my problem and seek the terms for its
solution (PK, 252).[21]

Polanyi recognizes that all human inquiry is conducted within
a fiduciary framework that is initially a-critically accepted by the
inquirer. But, if we are so wholly embedded in a particular tradition and time, how, despite our strivings to make contact with
reality, can we avoid sliding into subjectivism or relativism?

Overcoming the Subjective–Objective Divide

We have seen that Polanyi's position depends on his belief that an
external reality exists and that it is knowable. But our attempts to
establish contact with reality require acts of commitment. The
notion of commitment as a necessary condition for attaining
knowledge is an affront to those steeped in the ideal of objectivism.
"Epistemology has traditionally aimed at defining truth and falsity
in impersonal terms, for these alone are accepted as truly universal"
(PK, 303). It is precisely this ideal that Polanyi seeks to overturn. As
he explains it, the purpose of *Personal Knowledge* "is to re-equip
men with the faculties which centuries of critical thought have
taught them to distrust" (PK, 381). Objectivism seeks to remove the
human knower from the knowing process. But if all knowing is
either tacit or rooted in the tacit, then the participation of the
knower is an indispensable element in knowing, for the active
integration of the subsidiaries that produces the meaning of the

focal target takes place within the knower. If the participation of the knower is eliminated, no knowing can occur—or to put the matter slightly differently, "to avoid believing one must stop thinking" (PK, 314).

As we have seen, at the general level of language and culture, each person necessarily begins all inquiry within a fiduciary framework. But commitment occurs at yet another level. All assertions of fact implicitly carry with them the passionate commitment of the speaker. According to Polanyi, "if language is to denote speech it must reflect the fact that we never say anything that has not a definite impassioned quality" (PK, 27). Thus, a declaratory sentence, if it is to convey any meaning, must contain an implied prefix, which denotes "I believe."

> Such a prefix should not function as a verb, but as a symbol determining the modality of the sentence. The transposition of an assertion of fact into the "fiduciary mode" would correctly reflect the fact that such an assertion is necessarily attributable to a definite person at a particular place and time: for example, to the writer of the assertion at the moment of putting it to paper, or to the reader when he reads and accepts what is written (PK, 256).

This assertive quality of a declaratory sentence is what gives the sentence meaning. Thus, "an unasserted sentence is no better than an unsigned cheque; just paper and ink without power or meaning" (PK, 28).

If all declarations of fact imply an assertion of belief, then no truth claims can live up to the dispassionate objectivist ideal (PK, 256). The picture of the dispassionate thinker standing apart from the object of his attention and forcing it to submit to the universal laws of logical thought now appears to be clearly false. In truth, each individual participates passionately in the knowing process. This passionate knower asserts what he believes to be true, and in that assertion, he makes a claim about reality. But because reality is largely hidden and manifests itself in indeterminate, often unexpected ways, such a claim represents a commitment, for "a truthful statement commits the speaker to a belief in what he has asserted: he embarks in it on an open sea of limitless implications" (PK, 253).

Humans, of course, embark on this sea because we long for understanding. We possess an innate craving to make sense of chaos, to pursue the intimations of coherence that bear on a hidden reality that is waiting to be grasped (PK, 301; KB, 314, 316). This desire to understand is strong and motivates our passionate pursuit of knowledge. But when we believe we have grasped a truth, we also believe that the truth we have comprehended is of universal scope. If we believe that we have grasped a coherence bearing on reality, we "will expect it to be recognized by others" (SM, 36).[22] Polanyi calls this claim to universality "universal intent." Universal intent entails a claim about truth, for a truth claim is an assertion of what I believe to be true. Thus,

> an empirical statement is true to the extent to which it reveals an aspect of reality, a reality largely hidden to us, and *existing therefore independently of our knowing it.* By trying to say something that is true about a reality believed to be existing independently of our knowing it, all assertions of fact necessarily carry *universal intent. Our claim to speak of reality serves thus as the external anchoring of our commitment in making a factual statement* (PK, 311).

This claim of universal intent can embroil the individual in an unexpected tension. It frequently happens that a person makes a claim with universal intent only to realize that his position is not universally accepted. Polanyi writes: "We suffer when a vision of reality to which we have committed ourselves is contemptuously ignored by others. For a general unbelief imperils our own convictions by evoking an echo in us. Our vision must conquer or die" (PK, 150). Earlier we discussed the logical gap that must be crossed in an integrative act of illumination. Such an illumination represents a newly discovered coherence in reality, and since it bears on reality, the person who has traversed the gap will assert his newfound insight passionately and with universal intent. Polanyi terms this "persuasive passion." When impelled by it, the individual attempts to convert others to his way of thinking (PK, 150).

Polanyi's use of St. Augustine as a model for his postcritical epistemology makes it especially appropriate to speak in the idiom of conversion. While Augustine's famous conversion was a religious one and the type of conversion Polanyi discusses is primarily epistemological, the two are essentially the same. Whether in the religious or in the epistemological sense (and at times they may be one and the same), a conversion produces an alteration in one's fundamental interpretive framework. Such a "change" necessarily alters how one views the world. Conversions may entail a radical shift in one's interpretive framework or they may produce only a modest modification; the "depth of the cognitive commitment may be measured in either case by the ensuing change of our outlook" (PK, 318).

Conversion occurs when one's interpretive framework is challenged by that of another. In such cases, one encounters a new

conceptual language that produces a different interpretive framework, which in turn implies a "new way of reasoning" (PK, 151).
When opposing frameworks are so different that adherents of one
cannot even speak intelligibly to adherents of the other, the possibility of one partisan convincing another of the superiority of his
position is slight. But even when persuasion becomes impossible,
conversion remains viable (SFS, 81). Thus,

> the less two propositions have fundamentally in common the
> more the argument between them will lose its discursive charac-
> ter and become an attempt at mutually converting each other
> from one set of grounds to another, in which the contestants
> will have to rely largely on the general impressions of rationality
> and spiritual worth which they can make on one another. They
> will try to expose the poverty of their opponent's position and to
> stimulate interest for their own richer perspectives; trusting that
> once an opponent has caught a glimpse of these, he cannot fail
> to sense a new mental satisfaction, which will attract him further
> and finally draw him over to its own grounds (SFS, 66–67).

When a person's commitment to his interpretive framework is
shaken, he often experiences a "mental crisis which may lead to
conversion from one set of premises to another" (SFS, 67). But
such a movement is not completely specifiable, for

> conversion seems to come "out of the blue." It seems clear that
> we do not become converted—whether to a political party, a
> philosophy, *or* a religion—by having the truth of what we be-
> come converted to demonstrated to us in a wholly logical or

objective way. Rather, what happens when we become convinced is that we see at some point that the particular party or religion or epistemology or world view (or even scientific theory) in front of us holds possibilities for the attainment of richer meanings than the one we have been getting along with. At that moment we *are* converted, whether we have ever willed it or not (M, 179–80).[23]

Thus, epistemological conversion, like Augustine's religious conversion, occurs in some sense unexpectedly. That is not to say it cannot be desired, but in a real way it is a gift that arrives unbidden.[24] We tacitly come to dwell in subsidiaries that were either previously unknown or rejected. The integrations enabled by this new orientation produce new possibilities for meaning, and the increasing coherence attests to the contact with reality that has been attained.

The notion of universal intent, together with a commitment to the existence of an external reality, allows personal knowledge to overcome dualism between the objective and the subjective. As we have seen, Polanyi's main target in his epistemological writings is what he calls objectivism, which is shorthand for a collection of epistemological theories rooted in the thought of Descartes and Locke. The "crippling mutilations imposed by an objectivist framework," he tells us, have "totally falsified our conception of truth" (PK, 381, 286). It has been assumed that absolute objectivity is an attainable ideal and, consequently, that all knowledge based on belief is merely subjective (PK, 266). But aspiring to complete objectivity is a false and destructive ideal- a "Fool's Paradise" (PK, 268), which is ultimately self-contradictory for two reasons. First, "any attempt rigorously to eliminate our human perspective from our picture of the world must lead to absurdity" (PK, 3). This is true despite the fact that "the degree of our personal participation varies greatly within our various acts of knowing" (PK, 36). Thus, a theory of knowledge that fails to acknowledge the role played by the knower is logically impossible, and objectivism claims to do just that. Second, objectivism presumes that it is possible to construct a theory of knowledge apart from any belief. Attempting to rid itself of any a-critical elements, it accepts as knowledge only that which can be distinctly known and verified. But in reality, as we have seen, all knowledge depends on a fiduciary framework. While it is true that the objectivist claims to admit nothing as knowledge that depends on belief, it is more accurate to say that the objectivist "tolerates no *open* declaration of faith" (PK, 288, italics added). The contradiction in logic manifests itself in practice:

> I do not suggest, of course, that those who advocate philosophic doubt as a general solvent of error and a cure for all fanaticism would desire to bring up children without any rational guidance or contemplate any other scheme of universal hebetation. I am only saying that this would be what their principles demand. What they actually want is not expressed but concealed by their declared principles. They want their own beliefs to be taught to children and accepted by everybody, for they are convinced that this would save the world from error and strife (PK, 297).

In short, objectivism is fraught with contradictions. For these reasons, Polanyi rejects it.

But if the objectivist ideal is discarded, and replaced by Polanyi's theory of knowledge that emphasizes personal commitment and the fiduciary nature of all knowing, there is an obvious challenge: Does Polanyi's entire project rest on a circular argument? Polanyi makes this painfully clear when he sums up the implications of his account: "Any inquiry into our ultimate beliefs can be conducted only if it presupposes its own conclusions" (PK, 299). In other words, what Polanyi calls "our liberation from objectivism" (PK, 267) appears at first blush to be every bit as undesirable as what we have been liberated from. Polanyi realizes the inevitable criticism that his theory of knowledge will initially receive: "The moment such a programme is formulated it appears to menace itself with destruction. It threatens to sink into subjectivism: for by limiting himself to the expression of his own beliefs, the philosopher may be taken to talk only about himself" (PK, 299).

The key to solving the problem is to find a way to recognize the personal element in all knowing while at the same time affirming the objective nature of the thing known. In Polanyi's words,

we may distinguish between the personal in us, which actively enters into our commitments, and our subjective states, in which we merely endure our feelings. This distinction establishes the conception of the *personal*, which is neither subjective nor objective. In so far as the personal submits to requirements acknowledged by itself as independent of itself, it is not subjective; but in so far as it is an action guided by individual passions, it is not objective either. It transcends the disjunction between subjective and objective (PK, 300).

A key distinction between the merely subjective and the personal is the element of activity. While the subjective is passive and entails no passionate commitment, the personal "is neither an arbitrary act nor a passive experience, but a responsible act claiming universal validity" (PK, vii).[25] Here we see the centrality of Polanyi's realism, which combines with personal knowledge to keep his theory from descending into subjectivism. Personal commitment results from a passionate resolve to make contact with a hidden, though intimated, reality. We persistently strive to grasp the coherence of varied particulars, believing that they bear on a reality accessible to all knowers. Thus, personal knowledge "implies the claim that man can transcend his own subjectivity by striving passionately to fulfill his personal obligations to universal standards" (PK, 17).[26] In the sense that personal knowledge affirms the possibility of establishing contact with an independent, hidden reality, it is indeed objective knowledge (PK, vii). But since the passionate participation of the knower is ineliminable, knowing is never objective in the sense of being impersonal and completely unconditioned by the knower. "Subjective knowing is classed as passive; only knowing that bears on reality is active, personal, and rightly to be called objective" (PK, 403).

The active element of personal knowledge cannot be stressed enough, for this element determines whether a particular assertion is personal rather than subjective. Polanyi writes: "*The fiduciary passions which induce a confident utterance about the facts are **personal**, because they submit to the facts as universally valid, but when we reflect on this act non-committally its passion is reduced to **subjectivity**"* (PK, 303, italics and bold in original). In other words, if one passively reflects on a particular position, observing it, as it were, from the outside as a dispassionate and disengaged observer (the objectivist ideal), one is indeed speaking in terms of the subjective. But, if one passionately commits oneself to a position due to its perceived universality, which is a function of one's belief that contact with reality has been achieved, then the knowing is personal. If one looks *at* the position from the outside, it is subjective. If one looks from inside the position and all that it entails, and if one does so with universal intent, it is personal. The personal is a comfortable partner with the objective, while the subjective and the objective are mutually exclusive. Thus, personal knowledge overcomes the objective-subjective disjunction by affirming at once both the personal element in all knowing and the objective reality toward which all knowledge strives.

The Fact-Value Dichotomy

By transcending the subject-object barrier, Polanyi's theory has obvious implications for the so-called fact-value distinction.[27] If we agree with Polanyi that all knowing includes the personal participation of the knower and operates within a fiduciary framework, then it follows that all knowing—whether scientific or humane— is on the same epistemological footing. Thus, "the moment the ideal of detached knowledge was abandoned, it was inevitable that the ideal of dispassionateness should eventually follow, and that with it the supposed cleavage between dispassionate knowledge of fact and impassioned valuation of beauty should vanish" (SM, 38). The obvious conclusion is one that "denies any discontinuity between the study of nature and the study of man" (SM, 72).[28] This conclusion flies in the face of modern thought, which, in its attempt to protect science from all subjective elements, erected the fact-value barrier. But, in Polanyi's words, "it has now turned out that modern scientism fetters thought as cruelly as ever the churches had done. It offers no scope for our most vital beliefs and it forces us to disguise them in farcically inadequate terms" (PK, 265).[29] Polanyi offers his postcritical theory of knowledge in an attempt to give legitimate voice to those things we value most, despite the fact that they are not empirically verifiable.

The fact-value distinction is, as Polanyi argues, based upon a mistaken conception of the nature of knowing. If this is the case, then it follows that truth—which Polanyi defines as contact with an independent and hidden reality that manifests itself in the future in indeterminate and unexpected ways—is not the property solely of the empirical sciences. In his later work, Polanyi spoke in terms of "meaning," and this emphasis is clear as he describes the implications of breaking down the fact-value distinction:

> If . . . personal participation and imagination are *essentially* involved in science as well as in the humanities, meanings created in the sciences stand in no more favored relation to reality than do meanings created in the arts, in moral judgments, and in religion. At least they can stand in no more favored relation to reality on a basis of the supposed presence or absence of personal participation and imagination in the one rather than in the other. To have, or to refer to, reality—in some sense—may then be a possibility for both sorts of meanings, since the dichotomy between facts and values no longer

seems to be a real distinction upon which to hang any conclusions (M, 65).

By eliminating the distinction between facts and values, Polanyi
sought to reestablish the possibility for humans to embrace with
confidence such values as truth, beauty, and justice. These are not
merely subjective preferences; they are ideals to which we may
personally commit ourselves in the belief that they are truly
meaningful, for they bear on intangible reality. And that, as we have
seen, is actually more real than a reality that is merely tangible.[30]

It should be clear by now that Polanyi's theory of knowledge
descends neither into solipsism nor relativism. It is not solipsistic
because "it is based on a belief in an external reality and implies the
existence of other persons who can likewise approach the same
reality" (PK, 316).[31] And it is not relativistic because truth claims are
made with universal intent. They represent what "I believe to be
the truth, and what the consensus ought therefore to be" (PK, 316).[32]
While a theory of personal knowledge must admit "the indispensable biological and cultural rootedness of all free actions," it must
also acknowledge "that each man has some measure of direct access to the standards of truth and rightness and must limit for their
sake at some point his subjection to given circumstances" (SM, 89).

Because personal knowledge is not relativistic and is based on a
conception of truth grounded in reality, humans are not absolutely
free to do as they please. With freedom to know comes the responsibility to act in accordance with that knowledge. Objectivism, by
insisting on the ideal of detachment, "seeks to relieve us from all
responsibility for the holding of our beliefs" (PK, 323). Further-

more, by erecting the fact-value barrier, objectivism also greatly reduces the purview of our intellectual powers by seeking to dismiss all value judgments from the realm of knowledge. By insisting on the personal participation of the knower and by showing that all knowing includes a fiduciary element, Polanyi's theory produces a much broader venue for knowledge. But at the same time, the theory greatly reduces the knower's freedom from conditioning circumstances. In Polanyi's words: "This reappraisal demands that we credit ourselves with much wider cognitive powers than an objectivist conception of knowledge would allow, but at the same time it reduces the independence of human judgment far below that claimed traditionally for the free exercise of reason" (PK, 249).

As a realist, Polanyi affirms that truth is timeless. As real, however, truth may reveal itself in indeterminate future manifestations. Therefore, "though every person may believe something different to be true, there is only one truth" (PK, 315).[33] Further, what we claim to be true may conceivably be wrong, for "personal knowledge is an intellectual commitment, and as such inherently hazardous. Only affirmations that could be false can be said to convey objective knowledge of this kind" (PK, viii). Personal knowledge is risky; it requires a commitment to what we believe to be true, even though we may be wrong.[34] But our innate desire for coherence forces us to pursue what we cannot demonstrate with absolute certainty. Our passionate commitment to ideals we hold with universal intent establishes our responsibility. Our craving for the universal precludes arbitrary or glib choices: "*The freedom of the subjective person to do as he pleases is overruled by the freedom of the responsible person to do as he must*"

(PK, 309, italics in original). Thus, personal knowledge is a passionate commitment to universal truth made by limited, fallible knowers who strive to make contact with a hidden, indeterminate reality and embrace their findings with universal intent. In a provocative paragraph, Polanyi employs a theological analogy:

> The stage on which we thus resume our full intellectual powers is borrowed from the Christian scheme of Fall and Redemption. Fallen Man is equated to the historically given and subjective condition of our mind, from which we may be saved by the grace of the spirit. The technique of our redemption is to lose ourselves in the performance of an obligation which we accept, in spite of its appearing on reflection impossible of achievement. We undertake the task of attaining the universal in spite of our admitted infirmity, which should render the task hopeless, because we hope to be visited by powers for which we cannot account in terms of our specifiable capabilities (PK, 324).[35]

Our responsibility, then, is to ideals we cannot comprehend on the basis of our specifiable powers. But we pursue them nonetheless, because we believe that contact with reality is possible. And although we cannot articulate precisely how, we believe that our unspecifiable powers will propel us further than we can imagine. This hope, Polanyi adds, "is a clue to God" (PK, 324).

CHAPTER FOUR

MEANING, MORALITY, AND RELIGION

Meaning

In the previous chapter, we saw that at the heart of Polanyi's conception of knowing is his affirmation of a reality external to the knower, a reality that reveals itself unexpectedly in what Polanyi termed "indefinite future manifestations." This reality consists in both tangible and intangible elements; yet, as we saw, the intangibles are, in some respects, more real than the tangibles. The claim that intangible reality is more real, more meaningful, than tangible reality flies in the face of the materialistic reductionism that prevailed in the mid-twentieth century. An objectivist framework insisting that all knowledge must be explicitly verifiable is necessarily prejudiced in favor of a reductionist account of reality. This is clearly reflected in the analytical model of science best exemplified in Descartes' *Discourse on Method*, which seeks to break all objects of inquiry into their most fundamental parts. With the tools provided by an atomistic conception of the universe, reductionism became an approach to reality that views all things as reducible to physical properties. It claims to be capable of understanding all phenomena in terms of material forces.

Such a view of knowledge makes it impossible to make credible truth claims about such things as morality, aesthetics, or religion. These are necessarily relegated to the realm of purely subjective knowledge, but because knowledge *per se* must be explicit and verifiable, "subjective knowledge" is really an oxymoron. Subjective knowledge, in the world of objectivism, is more properly identified as a private feeling without any truth content whatsoever. As we have seen, Polanyi's goal in formulating a new account of knowing was to reintroduce the possibility of making meaningful truth claims about nonphysical reality. For Polanyi, the horrors of twentieth-century totalitarianism resulted directly from a critical framework that precludes at the outset any possibility of making meaningful moral claims. Polanyi's theory of tacit knowing opens the door to the very ideals that had been banished by a false view of knowledge. In the absence of those ideals, the world had been violently shaken. But moral ideals, while central to human existence, are not the only ones Polanyi's account of knowledge admits. His anti-reductionist theory of reality allows us to reconsider the very nature of nature and man's place in it. In order to provide an alternative to reductionist accounts of reality, Polányi worked long at developing an ontology according to which the fundamental laws of matter were given their due, but did not account for all of reality.

Modern reductionism has its roots in the new science of the early modern period. The mechanical philosophy of Galileo tended to describe all reality in terms of matter in motion. This view found its most extreme form in the materialistic reductionism suggested by the nineteenth-century French philosopher Pierre Simon Laplace. According to Laplace, a mind that could know at one time "all the forces by which nature is animated and the respective positions of the entities which compose it . . . would embrace in the same formula the movements of the largest bodies in the universe and those of the lightest atom: nothing would be uncertain for it, and the future, like the past, would be present to its eyes" (PK, 140). Theoretically the future and the past are perfectly predictable, if all reality can be reduced to matter acted upon by physical forces. Clearly, the notion of free will finds itself orphaned by such a conception— as does any meaningful conception of moral responsibility. Polanyi warns of the far-reaching effects of a reductionist conception of reality, for it is a harbinger of disorder for all intellectual pursuits. It is a "menace to all cultural values, including those of science, by an acceptance of a conception of man derived from a Laplacean ideal of knowledge and by the conduct of human affairs in the light of such a conception" (PK, 141).

The discovery of the structure of DNA by Watson and Crick allowed for an updated version of Laplace's reductionism, for in the view of many, all living things could now be understood in terms of physics and chemistry. Against such reductionism Polanyi argues that living things—indeed, even nonliving things such as machines—are fundamentally irreducible. For instance, if one sought to describe a watch in purely physical-chemical terms, what would one achieve? An atomic topography of the watch would not tell us what the watch is. We could never divine its function, its purpose, on the basis of this kind of analysis. The same applies to a book or any piece of printed matter. One cannot understand the meaning of a book merely by analyzing the physical-chemical structure of the paper and ink. For example, imagine that you have invented the watch; after building it you apply for a patent describing it purely in terms of its physical-chemical topography. Polanyi points out that "your patent would protect only the manufacture of an exact replica of your model. Your competitor could circumvent your patent by merely displacing one single atom of the patented topography. Only the principles underlying the operations of the watch in telling the time could specify your invention of the watch effectively, and these cannot be expressed in terms of physical-chemical variables" (SEP, 287). In order to comprehend the meaning of the watch, in order to understand the watch as a watch, we must understand its function. This being the case, Polanyi establishes that it is quite impossible adequately to describe machines or living beings without evoking the notion of teleology (KB, 157).

Reference to teleology has been frowned upon since the overthrow of the Aristotelian synthesis of the medieval schools. But Polanyi argues that it cannot be dispensed with so easily. "Even the most elaborate objectivist nomenclature cannot conceal the teleological character of learning and the normative intention of its study. Its supposedly objective terms still do not refer to purposeless facts but to well functioning things" (PK, 371–72). Scientists, Polanyi argues, find themselves attempting to do the impossible: speak of the function of a being without considering its purpose. This is nothing less than self-deception. "Everyone knows that you cannot inquire into the functions of living organisms without referring to the purpose served by them, and by the organs and processes which perform these functions. Yet we must pretend that all such teleological explanations are merely provisional. The story goes round among biologists that teleology is a woman of easy virtue, whom the biologist disowns in public, but lives with in private" (OMM, 16). But if all reality cannot be reduced to physics and chemistry, how are we to conceive of reality?

Polanyi describes a multi-leveled conception of reality grounded in physics and chemistry as the most basic principles but moving upward to increasingly higher principles. Think again of the watch: it is a machine, a human artifact used to harness the basic laws of nature to a particular end. Although the watch is constructed of physical materials, the human maker structures these materials according to the purpose intended for the machine. "So the machine as a whole works under the control of two distinct principles. The higher principle is that of the machine's design. This higher principle harnesses the lower one, which consists in the physicochemical process on which the machine relies for its working" (SEP, 300). We can see the distinction between these two principles if we imagine the machine being destroyed. The higher principle governing the machine's design would no longer be in effect vis à vis the machine, even though the lower principle governing the basic material would be maintained.

Each of these principles establishes what Polanyi, borrowing from physics, terms "boundary conditions." A boundary condition sets limits. As Polanyi puts it, "the boundary conditions of the physical-chemical changes taking place in a machine are the structural and operational principles of the machine. We say therefore that the laws of inanimate nature operate in a machine *under the control of operational principles that constitute* (or determine) *its boundaries*. Such a system is clearly under dual control" (SEP, 289, italics in original). Dual control represents the fact that each level is controlled both by its own laws and by the laws that control the comprehensive entity. This notion of dual control extends to any complex system:

> The laws of mechanics may be controlled by the operational principles which define a machine; the boundary conditions of muscular action may be controlled by a pattern of purposive behaviour, like that of going for a walk; the boundary of conditions of a vocabulary are usually controlled by the rules of grammar, and the conditions left open by the rules of chess are controlled by the stratagems of the players. And so we find that machines, purposive actions, grammatical sentences, and games of chess, are all entities subject to dual control (KB, 217).

This principle of dual control indicates that complex systems are actually stratified in a hierarchical fashion. We understand the meaning of a comprehensive entity only when we integrate the two levels of control conceptually. Thus, "smash up a machine, utter words at random, or make chess moves without a purpose, and the corresponding higher principle—that which constitutes the machine, that which makes words into sentences, and that which makes moves of chess into a game—will all vanish and the comprehensive entity which they controlled will cease to exist." But at the same time, the lower principles, the boundary conditions of which the now effaced higher principles had controlled, remain in operation. The laws of mechanics, the vocabulary sanctioned by the dictionary, the rules of chess, they will all continue to apply as before. Hence no description of a comprehensive entity in the light of its lower principles can ever reveal the operation of its higher principles. *The higher principles which characterize a comprehensive entity cannot be defined in terms of the laws that apply to its parts in themselves* (KB, 217).

Polanyi frequently illustrates this hierarchical structure of comprehensive entities by referring to the act of making a speech, which is a skill that requires the joining together of a number of levels into one comprehensive whole. At the lowest level, we see the most basic element necessary for giving a speech: the production of a voice. Next, we have the utterance of words. Then, there is the formation of words into sentences, followed by the arrangement of sentences into a particular style. Finally, there is the composition of the text itself. "The principles of each level operate under the control of the next higher level. The voice you produce is shaped into words by a vocabulary; a given vocabulary is shaped into sentences in accordance with grammar; and the sentences are fitted into a style, which in its turn is made to convey the ideas of the composition" (KB, 154). Dual control is evident at each level: the entity is subject both to the laws of its own level and to the laws of the next higher level. "Such multiple control is made possible by the fact that the principles governing the isolated particulars of a lower level, leave indeterminate their boundary conditions for the control by a higher principle. Voice-production leaves largely open the combination of sounds to words, which is controlled by a vocabulary. Next, a vocabulary leaves largely open the combination of words to form sentences, which is controlled by grammar; and so the sequence goes on" (KB, 154). Reductionism, therefore, is simply inadequate to account for the complex structure of comprehensive entities: "The operations of a higher level cannot be accounted for by the laws governing its particulars forming the next lower level. You cannot derive a vocabulary from phonetics; you cannot derive grammar from a vocabulary; a correct use of grammar does not account for good style; and good style does not provide the content of a piece of prose" (KB, 154–55). The content of the piece of prose, which is at once both the most complex and the least tangible of the levels, represents the integration of all the various levels into a coherent whole. If we rid ourselves of the bias toward identifying the tangible with the real, we easily recognize that the composition is a more complex reality than the lower levels. Polanyi's definition of reality as that which "may yet reveal itself to our deepened understanding in an indefinite range of unexpected manifestations" is helpful here, for when we define reality in these terms, the intangible suddenly appears more real than the tangible, for it promises a wider range of unexpected future manifestations.

This same hierarchical structure applies to living creatures as well as to machines and compositions:

all living functions rely on the laws of inanimate nature in controlling the boundary conditions left open by these laws; the vegetative functions sustaining life at its lowest levels leave open, both in plants and animals, the possibilities of growth and also leave open in animals the possibilities of muscular action; the

principles governing muscular action leave open their integration to innate patterns of behaviour; such patterns are open in
their turn to be shaped by intelligence, and the working of intelligence can be made to serve the still higher principles of man's
responsible choices (KB, 155).

Thus, while human existence is predicated upon the laws of physics
and chemistry, these laws do not prescribe the entirety of human
existence. Indeed, the higher levels are necessary to account fully for
human experience—an experience culminating in moral choices,
which represent one of the pinnacles of human achievement. In this
sense, the fullest meaning of human existence does not lie with the
lowest level of physics and chemistry but with the joint meaning of
all the levels, including moral and religious meaning, both of which
only emerge at the highest levels.

In this conception of reality, the Laplacean ideal—or any other
form of reductionism—is shown to be woefully inadequate.

*All meaning lies in higher levels of reality that are not reducible to
the laws by which the ultimate particulars of the universe are controlled.* The world view of Galileo, accepted since the Coperni-
can Revolution, proves fundamentally misleading. *What is most
tangible has the least meaning and it is perverse then to identify the
tangible with the real.* For to regard a meaningless substratum as
the ultimate reality of all things must lead to the conclusion
that all things are meaningless. And we can avoid this conclusion only if we acknowledge instead that deepest reality is possessed by higher things that are least tangible (OMM, 15).

Morality

Clearly, this view of reality bears directly on moral ideals—the very ideals Polanyi argues have been denied by a modern world dominated by a commitment to objectivism. Polanyi is confident that the moral skepticism inherent in objectivism cannot stand; just "as we know order from disorder, health from sickness, the ingenious from the trivial, we may distinguish with equal authority good from evil, charity from cruelty, justice from injustice" (STSR, 97). While Polanyi never systematically developed a moral theory, it is possible to sketch out a position from his writings. As we have seen, for Polanyi the intangible is more real than the tangible. And the real is defined as something independent of the knower, something that reveals itself in indeterminate and unpredictable ways. We come to know the real through a process of tacit integration—a process whereby the subsidiaries in which we dwell combine when we focus on a particular target to produce a meaning that is larger than the sum of the particulars. How does this theory of knowledge address the status of moral truth? Whereas modern objectivists believed that "the critical faculties of man unaided by any powers of belief could establish the truth of science and the canons of fairness, decency, and freedom" (SFS, 75), we have seen that all knowing depends on a fiduciary framework. Moral knowing is no exception. We come to accept moral teachings, like any other body of skillful knowing, by entrusting ourselves to a moral tradition or teacher in a process that is often referred to as interiorization. "To interiorize is to identify ourselves with the teachings in question, by making them function as the proximal term of a tacit moral knowledge, as applied in practice. This establishes the tacit framework for our moral acts and judgments" (TD, 17).

This description of the manner in which moral knowledge is acquired has certain implications. Since interiorization occurs within the human knower, it is correct to understand "man as the source of moral judgment and of all other cultural judgments by which man participates in the life of society" (SM, 28). But although tacit integration is achieved by the human knower, it does not follow that morality is an arbitrary invention of human beings. Since intangibles are more real than tangibles, the tacit integration that produces moral ideals actually elicits something more real than the physical world that sustains the knower in his physicality.

Because moral ideals are the product of tacit integration, they, like all integrations, bear on reality and are embraced with universal intent (PK, 214). This, of course, does not imply that moral standards are universally known. Personal knowledge, as we have seen, is inherently risky and carries with it the possibility that the truths embraced with universal intent may in fact be wrong. Thus, "values which I deem to be transcendent may be known only transiently to a small minority of mankind" (PK, 183). Furthermore, Polanyi believes that it is possible simply to deny the moral tradition into which one has been inculcated—as a result, for example, of commitment to a theory of knowledge that renders transcendent moral ideals impossible. Thus, Polanyi does "not assert that eternal truths are automatically upheld by men. We have learnt they can be very effectively denied by modern man" (SFS, 82–83).

Although moral reality can be denied, like scientific reality it has a status independent of the knower (PK, 242–43). In *Science, Faith and Society,* Polanyi refers to the truths that ought to direct our actions as "transcendent obligations." These include such ideals as truth, justice, and charity (SFS, 83).[1] Such truths cannot be derived as conclusions to a deductive argument. Instead, "belief in them can be upheld now only in the form of an explicit profession of faith" (SFS, 83). Moral ideals serve as subsidiaries in the active event of tacit knowing. As subsidiaries, they are largely unspecifiable when serving in that capacity:

> Indeed, we cannot look at our standards in the process of using them, for we cannot attend focally to elements that are used subsidiarily for the purpose of shaping the present focus of our attention. We attribute absoluteness to our standards, because by using them as part of ourselves we rely on them in the ultimate resort, even while recognizing that they are actually neither part of ourselves nor made by ourselves, but external to ourselves (PK, 183).

Moral ideals are real. Because they are real, they are characterized by indeterminate future manifestations. That is, the manner in which they might reveal themselves in the future may be completely unexpected. Moral ideals may change in the future as our contact with reality achieves new insights and greater coherence. But they will not change arbitrarily or explicitly. In the search for the solution to a problem, in the attempt to achieve greater coherence, we may alter our standards in practice in order to achieve that coherence. Thus, in seeking the solution to a problem "our intuition may respond to our efforts with a solution entailing new standards of coherence, new values. In affirming the solution, we tacitly obey these new values and thus recognize their authority over ourselves, over us who tacitly conceived them." This, Polanyi concludes, is "how new values are introduced, whether in science, or in the arts, or in human relations" (CI, 122).[2]

Religion

In 1944, J. H. Oldham, a distinguished ecumenical leader, invited Polanyi to join a group of leading thinkers who met on a regular basis to discuss basic questions facing Western civilization. Through these meetings, Polanyi came into contact with such figures as T. S. Eliot and Karl Mannheim, who were both members of the group. He was also exposed to the writings of theologians such as Paul Tillich and Reinhold Niebuhr. During his years of participation in the Moot, as the group called itself, Polanyi's theological and metaphysical ideas were developed and sharpened. There was a devotional element as well; the group worshipped together and began and ended each day with a brief prayer. During his time with the Moot, Polanyi was introduced to the Anglican Book of Common Prayer, which thereafter he carried in his breast pocket.[3] He regarded the biannual meetings of this group as a major influence on his thought. Referring to the intellectual stimulation and atmosphere of friendship he encountered there, he later observed that "these things changed our lives."[4] Indeed, Oldham is thanked in the acknowledgments of *Personal Knowledge* for having read and commented upon the entire manuscript.

There is no little controversy among Polanyi scholars regarding the development of his views on religious reality, as well as his own religious commitments. Nevertheless, a few things are clear. As we saw in the first chapter, Polanyi, a nonreligious Jew, converted to Roman Catholicism in 1919 just prior to his departure for Germany. Some have suggested that he converted more for practical than theological reasons. Membership in a Christian church likely did make life simpler for him. But his ongoing concern with religion, especially with Christianity, suggests more than a purely pragmatic conversion.[5]

Religion is a recurring theme in Polanyi's writing. And even where the religious implications are not made explicit, Polanyi clearly expected his audience to draw certain inferences. After a term at the School of Religion at Duke University, for example, Polanyi wrote Oldham: "The account I gave them in five lectures of my theory of knowledge and its consequences for our world outlook seems to have had a response from all parts of the university. I did not derive any religious or theological conclusions from my views, yet they were readily recognized by a number of ministers of religion who attended my talks."[6] Polanyi, though, often did attempt to make explicit the connections between his views and religion, for he was convinced that his theory of knowledge would reestablish the possibility of speaking meaningfully of religious truth. In the concluding paragraphs of *The Tacit Dimension*, Polanyi reflects on the very human need for "a purpose which bears on eternity." In light of the political and moral tragedies of the twentieth century, he states his belief that his theory of knowledge will remove the barriers created by an objectivist approach to knowledge: "Perhaps this problem cannot be resolved on secular grounds alone. But its religious solution should become more feasible once religious faith is released from pressure by an absurd vision of the universe, and so there will open up instead a meaningful world which could resound to religion" (TD, 92).

Yet another indication of his religious commitments is provided by Polanyi's having asked his friend Thomas Torrance, a Scottish theologian, to serve as his literary executor. According to Torrance, this was because Polanyi was disappointed with Harry Prosch, who—due to Polanyi's failing health—helped Polanyi turn several lectures into the book published as *Meaning*. According to Torrance, Prosch "had given a somewhat phenomenalist slant to Michael Polanyi's post-critical thought as a movement away from his critique of scientific objectivity, with a rather mystical view of Christianity, detached from the actual historical events and objectivity of the Christian message." Torrance explains that the reason Polanyi asked him to serve as his literary executor was to help ensure that the distortion that had occurred with *Meaning* would not happen again.[7] It should be noted in this regard that theologians, perhaps more than scholars in any other academic discipline, have been attracted to Polanyi's thought. Torrance, for example, was one of the first to recognize the fundamental importance of Polanyi's ideas.[8] The English missionary and churchman Leslie Newbigin has employed Polanyian concepts (along with those of Alasdair MacIntyre) in his work on Christian belief and pluralism.[9]

Quite apart from the compatibility of his ideas with religion, disagreement persists regarding Polanyi's personal beliefs. For example, Father Terence Kennedy, who has written on Polanyi's ideas in relation to theology, remarks that "honesty demands that we acknowledge that Polanyi was not religiously committed, nor did he have religious faith as this is understood in Christian theology."[10] On the other hand, Thomas Torrance writes, "as a rule Michael Polanyi was rather reticent about discussing his own religious beliefs, for some of his ardent supporters in the philosophy of science, like Marjorie Grene, were . . . rather hostile to religion." Despite this reticence, Torrance notes that "Michael Polanyi, as I knew him, was certainly a Christian." He recounts that, in the last letter he received from Polanyi, "he wrote about the visit he and Magda had paid to Guildford Cathedral to celebrate Easter, where in their worship he was overwhelmed with the actual resurrection of Christ."[11] Another Polanyi friend, Lady Drusilla Scott, quotes from a letter Polanyi sent her on the subject of religion. Polanyi wrote, "I am of course aiming at the foundation of religious faith. Have been doing so since I started thinking about matters in general twenty-five years ago. But I became increasingly reticent about this as time went on."[12]

Was Polanyi reluctant to speak openly about his religious convictions for pragmatic reasons, in order to avoid the accusation that his project was merely a way to bring religion in through the back door? Possibly. On the other hand, his reticence could have been the product of doubt. Polanyi's long friendship with J. H. Oldham reveals some of this ambivalence. Oldham seemed convinced that Polanyi was, indeed, a Christian. In 1947, he invited Polanyi to a meeting of friends "to advise us how, in the next year or two, we can write most helpfully about God (directly or indirectly) in the Christian News Letter, and about the roads that lead to Him."[13] In 1948, while planning a meeting of the Moot to discuss modern atheism and the Christian belief in God, Oldham wrote to Polanyi that "we should, if possible, have one or two non-Christians in the group, provided we can find the right people."[14] Polanyi's response to Oldham's suggestion clearly reveals his discomfort: "Our meetings leave me increasingly with the feeling that I have no right to describe myself as a Christian. So perhaps I may feel the part of the outsider in the discussion."[15] As early as 1934 (soon after moving to England) he wrote to a friend: "I do not doubt that science and Catholicism can be united in one mind. Quantum mechanics are certainly more difficult to believe than Catholic faith. But I bring myself to believe quantum mechanics. I need them. I think I should believe them. I have not the same feeling, the same urge towards Catholicism." Polanyi then goes on to note his discomfort with the Catholic Church's involvement in the mistreatment of the Jews in Hungary as well as with its abuses of power during the Spanish Inquisition. Additionally, in his opinion, the Church had shown only a grudging support for the pursuit of scientific discovery. "The whole adventure of practical reasoning, I feel, is only tolerated by the Church. I think it is a vital mission of humanity to push on this adventure. If you forgive me, I would say, God has ordained this adventure to us."[16] Indeed, his discussions of Christianity in his philosophic writings appear to be oriented toward Protestant theology. On this point, he writes, "I find my own conception of the scope and method of a progressive Protestant theology confirmed by many passages in the writings of Paul Tillich" (PK, 283 n.1). Torrance, incidentally, reports that Polanyi eventually distanced

himself from Tillich's work. Nevertheless, Polanyi's explicitly theological passages seem generally Protestant in flavor.[17]

Religion in Personal Knowledge

Regardless of Polanyi's own personal religious commitments, his
writing frequently touches on religious belief and specifically on
Christianity. *Personal Knowledge* contains two sustained discussions of religion. But before we turn to these, it might be useful to
point out that, in keeping with his theory of tacit knowing, which
relies on a from-to structure, religious belief (along with justice,
morality, and art) cannot be meaningfully analyzed by atomizing
its elements. For example, the word "justice" is not meaningful in
any comprehensive sense as a focal object. Instead "we must look,
intently and discriminatingly, *through* the term 'justice' at justice
itself, this being the proper use of the term 'justice,' the use which
we want to define. To look instead *at* the word 'justice' would only
destroy its meaning" (PK, 116). Polanyi's distinction between looking through and looking at is reminiscent of a similar distinction
made by C. S. Lewis in a short essay titled "Meditation in a Tool
Shed."[18] In this piece, Lewis recounts his experience of standing in
a dark shed on a sunny day. Through a crack shines a sunbeam. As
Lewis examines the beam of light, he notices the dust particles
floating silently in it and the dim outline of the interior of the shed.
As he shifts his position so that he now looks along the beam, the
beam itself disappears and he sees the world outside the shed. This
suggests to Lewis that there are two ways of looking at an object or
an idea. First, one can look at the thing from the outside, as it were.

One can seek an objective and impersonal position from which to observe, but from this vantage one will never know all that can be known about the object or idea. To know it more fully, one must be willing to employ a second kind of looking that is from within or, as Lewis puts it, "looks along." To look along, one must forfeit one's outside perspective and submit oneself to the strictures of the thing or idea. Modern man, in his obsessive pursuit of objective certainty, has rejected the second kind of looking as merely subjective. Lewis argues that true knowing must be open to both kinds of looking; to ignore one or the other is to produce a truncated view of reality. Polanyi, in the same way, argues that this insight is crucial for achieving a fully human existence; the highest achievements of a person will dissolve "if he turns his back and examines what he respects in a detached manner. Then law is no more than what the courts will decide, art but the emollient of nerves, morality but a convention, tradition but inertia, God but a psychological necessity. Then man dominates a world in which he himself does not exist. For with his obligations he has lost his voice and his hope, and been left behind meaningless to himself" (PK, 380).

With this distinction between looking at and looking along established, we turn now to the two extended discussions of religion in *Personal Knowledge*. The first comes in a section titled "Dwelling In and Breaking Out." We saw in the last chapter that indwelling is an essential element of knowing. It is through indwelling a tool or an idea or a conceptual framework that we appropriate it and thereby incorporate it as an extension of our mental capacities. Polanyi argues that humans seek satisfaction by "gaining intellectual control over the external world," and that this is accomplished by constructing and dwelling in a satisfying conceptual framework. Yet, the urge to push our understanding of the world further has the effect of destroying the frameworks in which we dwell. The succession of scientific theories demonstrates this point clearly: when it breaks out of one conceptual framework, "the mind is for the moment directly experiencing its content rather than controlling it by the use of any pre-established modes of interpretation; it is overwhelmed by its own passionate activity" (PK, 196). This urge continually to push beyond what we know, to break out of our fixed conceptual frameworks, is evidence of "our craving for mental dissatisfaction" (PK, 196).

In religious terms, this breaking out is represented by worship. "The Christian faith in everyday action is just such a sustained effort at breaking out, sustained by the love and desire for God, a God who can be loved but not observed. Proximity to God is not an observation, for it overwhelms and pervades the worshipper" (PK, 198). Attempting to observe God is analogous to looking at the beam of sunlight in order to see the sun: the reality will be invisible. When one ceases to observe from the outside and through an act of worship submits to the divine reality, one experiences God. As Polanyi puts it, "the religious ritual . . . is potentially the highest degree of indwelling that is conceivable," for the Christian act of worship incorporates one's entire body and mind in an act of submission. Nevertheless, the worshipper does not enjoy this act of indwelling, for "the confession of guilt, the surrender to God's mercy, the prayer for grace, the praise of God, bring about mounting tension." Through worship, the Christian becomes aware of his guilt and prayerfully hopes for the gift of divine mercy. "The ritual of worship is expressly designed to induce and sustain this state of anguish, surrender and hope" (PK, 198). Because the act of Christian worship has no final consummation in this world, the indwelling of the Christian through worship is, "a continued attempt at breaking out, at casting off the condition of man, even while humbly acknowledging its inescapability" (PK, 198). Unlike the breaking out of the scientist, who then indwells a new scientific theory, the Christian will never succeed in a similar movement. "Christian worship sustains, as it were, an eternal, never to be consummated hunch." Yet this eternal hunch is, ultimately, satisfying: "Christianity sedulously fosters, and in a sense permanently satisfies, man's craving for mental dissatisfaction by offering him the comfort of a crucified God" (PK, 199).

While both the scientist and the Christian worshipper indwell particular conceptual frameworks from which they strive to break out, it is clear that the scientist's work bears more directly on the facts of experience than do the acts of the worshipper. Thus, according to Polanyi it is proper to speak of scientific verification, whereas religion, and also art, are tested and accepted by a process of validation.

> Our personal participation is in general greater in a validation than in a verification. The emotional coefficient of assertion is intensified as we pass from the sciences to the neighboring domains of thought. But both *verification* and *validation* are everywhere an acknowledgment of a commitment: they claim the presence of something real and external to the speaker. As distinct from both of these, *subjective* experiences can only be

said to be *authentic*, and authenticity does not involve a commitment in the sense in which both verification and validation do (PK, 202).

To put this distinction in the terms suggested by C. S. Lewis, verification can be achieved by looking at, while validation is achieved only by looking along.

The distinction between those truths which can be tested and accepted by verification and those which are held by validation is pursued in a later section titled "Religious Doubt." In Polanyi's view, it is incorrect to argue for the existence of God in some purely dispassionate fashion. "God cannot be observed, any more than truth or beauty can be observed. He exists in the sense that He is to be worshipped and obeyed, but not otherwise; not as a fact—any more than truth, beauty or justice exist as facts. All these, like God, are things which can be apprehended only in serving them" (PK, 279). In other words, a scientific claim can rightfully be called a fact, for it can be verified. On the other hand, religious claims, like other claims not rooted directly in empirical experience, are validated by virtue of participating in them, by looking along them rather than looking at them. As Polanyi puts it, "the Christian enquiry is worship" (PK, 281). Thus, attempts to demonstrate the truth of a miracle, for instance, serve to undermine the articulate structure one indwells by virtue of worship. Thinkers such as David Hume attacked the belief in miracles by arguing that there is no evidence to support the claims of believers.[19] Yet, Polanyi argues, "if the conversion of water into wine or the resuscitation of the dead could be experimentally verified, this would strictly disprove their miraculous nature. Indeed, to the extent to which any event can be established in the terms of natural science, it belongs to the natural order of things. However monstrous and surprising it may be, once it has been fully established as an observable fact, the event ceases to be regarded as supernatural" (PK, 284).

The modern prejudice in favor of dispassionate knowing, characterized by "looking at," has rendered impossible (or at best problematic) the claims of religious belief. By pointing out the personal nature of knowing—the validation that only occurs by looking along—Polanyi has opened the door for a reaffirmation of religious belief. As he puts it: "Today we should be grateful for the prolonged attacks made by rationalists on religion for forcing us to renew the grounds of the Christian faith" (PK, 286). Objectivism, which insists that all which cannot be verified must be doubted, has undermined the very things we, as humans, hold most dear. It

> has totally falsified our conception of truth, by exalting what we can know and prove, while covering up with ambiguous utterances all we can know and *cannot* prove, even though the latter knowledge underlies, and must ultimately set its seal to, all that we *can* prove. In trying to restrict our minds to the few things that are demonstrable, and therefore explicitly dubitable, it has overlooked the a-critical choices which determine the whole being of our minds and has rendered us incapable of acknowledging these vital choices (PK, 286).

Faith and Reason

Polanyi's theory of knowledge has, he believes, important implications for the relationship of faith and reason. In a 1961 essay, Polanyi argues that, while faith and reason have since the inception of philosophy been distinguished conceptually, modern rationalism has made a stronger claim by insisting that reason alone is capable of determining true knowledge. Thus, "faith was no longer to be respected as a source of higher light, revealing knowledge that lies beyond the range of observation and reason, but was to be regarded merely as a personal acceptance which falls short of rational demonstrability" (FR, 238). Modern scientism has undermined the possibility of making truth claims that extend beyond the dominion of science. As we have seen, the moral and political repercussions have been enormous. Polanyi seeks to restore faith to its proper place by showing how it is central to the knowing process.

Tacit knowing, as we have seen, involves the integration of two distinct elements: the focal and the subsidiary. As Polanyi puts it, "there are two kinds of knowing which invariably enter jointly into any act of knowing a comprehensive entity. There is (1) the knowing of a thing by attending to it, in the way we attend to an entity as a whole, and (2) the knowing of a thing by relying on our awareness of it, in the way we rely on our awareness of the particulars forming the entity for attending to it as a whole" (FR, 239). As soon as we speak of relying on something in order to comprehend something else, we begin to see the role faith necessarily plays in the knowing process. One cannot critically assess subsidiary clues while attending to the focal target. Instead, one must hold the subsidiaries a-critically in order to know the object of one's attention. And even if one attempts to shift one's attention to the subsidiaries, a coherent knowing of these necessarily depends on our reliance on other subsidiaries. Thus, at the heart of the knowing process lies an ineradicable act of faith. This is clear whether we rely on a tool to perform a particular function, on a word to convey a particular meaning, or on an authority to transmit a certain skill. As Polanyi puts it, "the traditional division between faith and reason, or faith and science . . . reflects the assumption that reason and science proceed by explicit rules of logical deduction or inductive generalization." On the contrary, scientific knowing entails what Polanyi termed "the unaccountable element." More broadly, if all knowing consists in the tacit integration of subsidiaries into focal objects, then knowing is not a simple process of applying explicit rules to produce a specified outcome. "To know is to understand, and explicit logical processes are effective only as tools in search of the solution of a problem, commitment by which we expand our understanding and continue to hold the result. They have no meaning except within this informal dynamic context. Once this is recognized, the contrast between faith and reason dissolves, and the close similarity of this structure emerges in its place" (FR, 244).

The modern insistence on the ideal of pure objectivity has, in Polanyi's words, destroyed "the I-Thou commitment of the religious world view and establish[ed] a panorama of I-It relations in its place" (FR, 245). Yet, when the world is thus reduced, the human does not escape. Thus, we see scientists attempting to describe the totality of human activity in purely mechanistic terms.

In actuality, we do not know other minds by observing the particulars of which they are composed (as if a neural surgeon could grasp the totality of another mind by cutting into the brain and observing it); instead, we know other minds by dwelling in their manifestations. "Such is the structure of empathy (which I prefer to call conviviality), which alone can establish a knowledge of other minds—and even of the simplest living beings" (FR, 245). Conviviality is the opposite of the modern ideal of detached impersonality. But where the ideal of detachment reduces the world to a mere series of appetites or a machine,

> the kind of knowledge which I am vindicating here, and which I call *personal knowledge*, casts aside these absurdities of the current scientific approach and reconciles the process of knowing with the acts of addressing another person. In doing so, it establishes a continuous ascent from our less personal knowing of inanimate matter to our convivial knowing of living beings and beyond this to the knowing of our responsible fellow men. Such I believe is the true transition from science to the humanities and also from our knowing the laws of nature to our knowing the person of God (FR, 245).

In the context of Polanyi's theory of knowledge, "natural knowing expands continuously into knowledge of the supernatural" (FR, 246).

Polanyi, as usual, looks to scientific discovery as a paradigmatic example of this transition beyond natural knowing. As we have seen, the scientist is guided by his passion for a problem coupled by his intuition that a solution is at hand. He is committed to the belief that reality can be known truly, albeit imperfectly.

Although he has no explicit rules to apply, he nevertheless gropes for a solution.

> The discoverer must labor night and day. For though no labor can make a discovery, no discovery can be made without intense, absorbing, devoted labor. Here we have a paradigm of the Pauline scheme of faith, works and grace. The discoverer works in the belief that his labors will prepare his mind for receiving a truth from sources over which he has no control. I regard the Pauline scheme therefore as the only adequate conception of scientific discovery (FR, 246–47).

Thus, faith and reason are shown to be fundamentally interdependent. To deny one in preference of the other is to produce a fundamentally incoherent, not to say destructive, account of knowing. By reestablishing the centrality of faith, Polanyi has destroyed the modern objectivist ideal. And he has thereby cleared the way for a reintroduction of God into the realm of true knowing.

Science and Religion

As we saw at the beginning of this chapter, Polanyi seeks to counter materialistic reductionism with his account of a stratified ontology. He borrows the notion of boundary conditions from the language of physics and shows how each level of a machine or an organism is subject to dual control. Polanyi develops this account to show how the theory of evolution, if conceived purely in terms of natural selection and random mutations, is inadequate. In a 1963 article titled "Science and Religion: Separate Dimensions or Common

Ground?" Polanyi introduces the subject by dissenting from Paul Tillich's notion (in some ways similar to Steven Jay Gould's more recent idea of nonoverlapping magisteria)[20] that science and religion occupy two completely separate domains, and if each would merely stick to its own business, no conflict would arise. As Polanyi paraphrases Tillich, "science and religion would speak then in two different dimensions which logically by-pass each other, the dimension of science being that of strictly detached knowledge, while the dimension of religion is one of unconditional commitment" (SR, 4). As we have seen, Polanyi, in his attempt to show that completely detached knowledge is impossible, rejects such a description of the cleavage between science and religion.[21]

The core problem is the modern ideal of strict detachment. If all knowledge includes the personal participation of the knower, then the ideal of strict detachment is false. And clearly, if this ideal is a false one, science and religion stand on similar grounds—or better, they stand on a continuum, with one leading naturally to the other.

The ideal of strict detachment has led to a reductionist view of reality. But when all reality is conceived in terms of materiality, the scientist who subscribes to this view will believe that his subject matter can be represented purely in terms of physics and chemistry. This mistaken view results in an absurdity and a subtle error. The absurdity is the claim that "the sentience of animals and the experience of consciousness in general can be accounted for by the laws of physics and chemistry" (SR, 9). As Polanyi notes, this view has led some scientists to deny the very existence of consciousness. The subtle error is this: when a biologist, for example, claims that all living systems can be conceived in terms of physics and chemistry, "the purpose that biology actually pursues, and by which it achieves its triumphs, consists in explaining living beings in terms of *a mechanism founded on the laws of physics and chemistry, but not determined by them*" (SR, 10, italics in original). We have returned now to Polanyi's notion of boundary conditions and a hierarchical conception of reality. Taking this account of reality in conjunction with his theory of knowledge, Polanyi believes we can establish a better understanding of the human condition. As he puts it, we must not allow the ideal of strict detachment to

> deprive our image of man and the universe of any rational foundation. All men, scientists included, must seek and hold on to a reasonable view of the universe and of man's place in it. For acquiring this we must rely on a theory of knowledge which accepts indwelling as the proper way for discovering and possessing the knowledge of comprehensive entities. I believe also that this may open up a cosmic vision which will harmonize with some basic teachings of Christianity (SR, 11).

In seeking this cosmic vision that provides a meaningful world in which both science and religion take their rightful places, "we should turn in the first place to common sense" (SR, 11). Common sense tells us that we are conscious beings. Common sense tells us that our lives and the lives of others matter. Common sense tells us that beauty and truth and justice exist, however imperfect their temporal manifestations. In other words, we must expand our conception of reality beyond the strictures of materialism in order fully to account for human experience. As for human origins,

The book of Genesis and its great pictorial illustrations, like the frescoes of Michelangelo, remain a far more intelligent account of the nature and origin of the universe than the representations of the world as a chance collocation of atoms. For the biblical cosmology continues to express—however inadequately—the significance of the fact that the world exists and that man has emerged from it, while the scientific picture denies any meaning to the world, and indeed ignores all our most vital experience of this world. The assumption that the world has some meaning which is linked to our own calling as the only morally responsible beings in the world, is an important example of the supernatural aspect of experience which Christian interpretations of the universe explore and develop (PK, 284–85).

The neo-Darwinist version of evolution, which is based on the twin mechanisms of natural selection and random mutation, is inadequate in Polanyi's view. Its inadequacy is not readily apparent due to "a fundamental vagueness inherent in this theory which tends to conceal its inadequacy." This inadequacy is rooted in the fact that "we lack any acceptable conception of the way in which genic changes modify ontogenesisa—a deficiency, which is due in its turn to the fact that we can have no clear conception of living beings, as long as we insist on defining life in terms of physics and chemistry" (PK, 383). If natural selection is inadequate, then we must locate another mechanism or force by which evolution operates. Polanyi posits that

> the *ordering principle* which *originated* life is the *potentiality* of a stable open system; while the inanimate matter on which life feeds is merely a *condition* which *sustains* life, and the accidental

configuration of matter from which life had started had merely *released* the operations of life. And evolution, like life itself, will then be said to have been *originated* by the *action* of an ordering principle, an action *released* by random fluctuations and *sustained* by fortunate *environmental conditions* (PK, 383–84).

By using and emphasizing words like the "ordering principle" which "originated" and "sustains" life, Polanyi clearly speaks in terms that are not reducible to pure materialistic causes. Of course such language is redolent of the vitalist philosophies of Henri Bergson or Pierre Teilhard de Chardin. But as Polanyi puts it, "it is obvious . . . that the rise of man can be accounted for only by other principles than those known today to physics and chemistry. If this be vitalism, then vitalism is mere common sense, which can be ignored only by a truculently bigoted mechanistic outlook" (PK, 390).[22]

Life is an achievement. Human life—characterized by consciousness, curiosity, creativity, and moral responsibility—represents the apex of this achievement. Bound up within the meaning of human existence is our duty, as individual centers of thought and responsibility, to employ our faculties to live lives worthy of our cosmic calling. Polanyi concludes *Personal Knowledge* with the following observation on the position of man in the cosmos: "We may envisage then a cosmic field which called forth all these centres by offering them a short-lived, limited, hazardous opportunity for making some progress of their own towards an unthinkable consummation. And that is also, I believe, how a Christian is placed when worshipping God" (PK, 405).

CHAPTER FIVE

ENGAGING POLANYI IN THE TWENTIETH CENTURY AND BEYOND

WITH AN OVERVIEW OF the main strands of Polanyi's thought in place, we will conclude by considering his views in the context of other twentieth-century thinkers. Of course, because Polanyi wrote extensively on a broad range of topics, any brief comparison is bound to be incomplete and at best suggestive of possible lines of inquiry. Nevertheless, in what follows I hope to provide some idea of the ways his thought parallels that of some of his contemporaries. Additionally, I want briefly to suggest how Polanyi's ideas might prove helpful, not merely for understanding the twentieth century, but the twenty-first as well.

While it is correct to situate Polanyi's work in the broad context of classical liberalism, he was no apologist for *laissez-faire* capitalism. He believed there is a proper and necessary role for government, and that this extends well beyond the minimalist "night-watchman" state. Polanyi also consistently and actively opposed communism and fascism. Having recognized the moral vacuum at the heart of twentieth-century totalitarianism, he dedicated himself to articulating an approach to knowing that would once again make belief in moral and religious truth possible.

Although he was an outspoken opponent of communism, Polanyi did not identify strongly with the postwar conservative movement. To be sure, many of his ideas have been embraced by conservatives, which is not surprising, since they offer powerful philosophical support for certain strands of conservative thought. In 1964, after Polanyi decided not to renew his subscription to *National Review*, William F. Buckley Jr. wrote him personally: "All of us here had hoped you had found us useful during the past year; the disappointment, as I say, is keen. *National Review* can ill afford to lose you; nor, for that matter, can the whole movement for an enlightened conservatism."[1] Several years later, Buckley invited Polanyi to write for *National Review*. Polanyi's reply indicates that he had some reservations about Buckley's enterprise:

> I was glad to hear from you and to be invited to write for the *National Review*. I have just been reading your collection of essays entitled "Up from Liberalism" and I am wondering how far I agree with you.
>
> I think I do in many ways, but somehow I feel the times have passed for this battle. I wish I could show you that, but I have no chance of writing about it now. I must follow up certain tasks, which I must not set aside, however tempting the alternative would be.
>
> So it remains to thank you and to retain the pleasure of having made contact with you, in the hope that one day I might find something to say in response to your work, or at least on grounds akin to those you are developing.[2]

Although Polanyi apparently doubted whether his ideas ran parallel to those of American conservatives, his theory of knowledge nevertheless includes a sophisticated and appreciative account of tradition, authority, practice, and community—elements central to conservative thought. As we have seen, Polanyi had great affection for Edmund Burke. Indeed, he claimed that the progress dreamed of by Burke's opponents could only be pursued in the context of "the kind of traditionalism taught by . . . Edmund Burke" (TD, 63). Polanyi read carefully Richard Weaver's *Ideas have Consequences*, one of the primary articulations of American conservatism, and Edward Shils, author of a book titled *Tradition*, was one of only four people whom Polanyi thanked for having commented on the manuscript of *Personal Knowledge*. Shils, for his part, wrote Polanyi that "*Personal Knowledge* has become sort of part of my mental furniture."[3]

In the late 1960s and early 1970s Polanyi corresponded with Daniel Patrick Moynihan. When the correspondence began, Moynihan was assistant to President Nixon. He was especially impressed with Polanyi's 1960 article "Beyond Nihilism." After he gave the commencement address at the University of Notre Dame in 1969, Moynihan received a letter from Polanyi:

> There is a great deal I want to tell you in reply to your commencement speech at Notre Dame. Let me say at the moment only that I feel a kinship with you to which I attach great hopes.
>
> I sent you by air a copy of "Knowing and Being" which includes the essay "Beyond Nihilism." I think you were the first to mention it in public.[4]

A central theme in "Beyond Nihilism" is moral inversion, and Moynihan found that concept particularly useful for understanding the radical politics of the day. On at least two occasions, Moynihan sent Polanyi news articles describing horrific acts of excess that, to his mind, were best understood as examples of moral inversion. In response to one such letter containing an article on the radical group that called itself "the Weathermen," Polanyi wrote:

> The article by Kifner on Weathermen is profoundly revealing and I understand why you sent it to me.
>
> I have spent much of the time since January on composing an essay on the nature and history of moral inversion, and had you in mind while doing so.[5]

In response to Polanyi's 1970 article "Science and Man," which recapitulates the main points of his thought, Moynihan wrote enthusiastically to Polanyi: "I am utterly enthralled by 'Science and Man.' Brilliant—provocative—true."[6]

Although he was reluctant to be labeled, Polanyi's ideas clearly resonated with many social commentators in the years following World War II. Likewise, he frequently wrote in terms congenial to Christianity, and he recognized and approved of the religious implications of his thought, yet he was at best ambivalent about orthodox Christianity. Where then, does that leave our understanding of Michael Polanyi? How can we locate his work in the larger context of the twentieth century and beyond?

In what follows, I want first to situate Polanyi in reference to three other twentieth-century thinkers, and then to point out how his thought can help move us beyond both Enlightenment rationalism and postmodern skepticism.

Michael Oakeshott

The British political philosopher Michael Oakeshott (1901–90) found much in Polanyi's writings with which to agree. Although Polanyi never refers to Oakeshott in print, he was aware of his work. (There are, in fact, several quotations from Oakeshott in Polanyi's collected papers.) Oakeshott, by contrast, mentioned Polanyi on several occasions, although his only sustained discussion of Polanyi appears in a review of *Personal Knowledge*.[7] Widely regarded as a fine prose stylist, Oakeshott criticizes Polanyi's presentation:

> It is a book full of side-glances into other matters; it is disordered, repetitive, digressive, and often obscure; as a work of art it leaves much to be desired. . . . Professor Polanyi's ambition to let nothing go by default, to surround his argument with an embroidery, not of qualification but of elaboration, and to follow his theme into every variation that suggests itself, make the book like a jungle through which the reader must hack his way.[8]

Yet despite the stylistic shortcomings, Oakeshott finds much to appreciate in the book. He notes with favor Polanyi's critique of empiricism, his denial of the moral neutrality of scientific investigation, and his insistence on the personal element in all knowing. Oakeshott agrees that scientific knowing is an acquired skill—one obtained through practice and including an unspecifiable element that cannot be reduced to rules.

Oakeshott nonetheless does detect a possible problem in Polanyi's theory of knowledge: once absolute objectivity is denied, he worries, the danger of a slide into subjectivism becomes acute. Although Polanyi goes to great lengths to respond to this objection, Oakeshott is unsure of his ultimate success. He rightly understands that Polanyi's theory of knowledge escapes subjectivism only if Polanyi's realism is true. Thus, Oakeshott writes, "in the end a belief that our thoughts are moved by 'an innate affinity for making contact with reality' seems to be the only premiss, properly speaking, of scientific enquiry and the means by which it transcends merely personal conviction."[9] Oakeshott, a self-proclaimed skeptic,[10] muses that this premise seems to rest on excessive belief, for Polanyi's theory of knowledge "is as little skeptical as it is positivistic . . . [and] . . . Professor Polanyi doesn't do as much skepticism for himself as might have been hoped and as the occasion seems to demand."[11] Oakeshott goes on to suggest that Polanyi's lack of a skeptical demeanor indicates that "at the edges of his argument there is a suspicion of philosophical innocence."[12] This criticism should not surprise us. After all, Oakeshott once wrote that "it is always more difficult to doubt radically and intelligently than to believe."[13] Here, at the very foundations of their respective theories of knowledge, a twofold disagreement emerges, which in large measure sums up the differences between these two thinkers: Oakeshott is an idealist, whereas Polanyi is a realist. Oakeshott is also a skeptic, whereas Polanyi promotes an a-critical philosophy.[14]

Despite these fundamental differences, Oakeshott finds much in Polanyi's writings with which to agree. In his seminal essay, "Rationalism in Politics," Oakeshott discusses two types of knowledge—practical and technical. Technical knowledge is required for every scientific or practical endeavor, and "its chief characteristic is that it is susceptible of precise formulation, although special skill and insight may be required to give it that formulation."[15] Practical knowledge, on the other hand, "exists only in use, is not reflective and (unlike technique) cannot be formulated in rules."[16] Oakeshott remarks in a footnote that "some excellent observations on this topic are to be found in M. Polanyi, *Science, Faith and Society*."[17] In another essay, Oakeshott points the reader's attention to the same work by Polanyi and calls it "brilliant."[18] Oakeshott obviously found much common ground between his emphasis on practical knowledge and Polanyi's discussion of the process of scientific investigation.[19] In Polanyi's words, "the rules of research cannot be usefully codified at all. Like the rules of all other high arts, they are embodied in practice alone" (SFS, 33).

For both men, knowledge embodied in practice cannot be acquired except through a personal relationship between a master and an apprentice. Submitting himself to the authority of the master, the apprentice acquires the skills necessary to master his particular field of inquiry. Such knowledge exists only in traditions, which exercise authority by requiring a degree of submission from those who seek to become full practicing members.[20] Thus, Oakeshott's practical knowledge is quite similar to the unformulatable knowledge of which Polanyi speaks. Furthermore, Oakeshott insists that the modern rationalist relies excessively on technical knowledge while denying practical knowledge. This parallels the philosophical disposition Polanyi calls "objectivism."[21] Finally, both believe that a central problem with modern politics is the erroneous theory of knowledge that lies at its base. In Oakeshott's understanding, the modern rationalist, in his zealous quest for rational certainty, denies any knowledge that is not technical, that cannot be formulated into explicit rules.[22] Similarly, Polanyi argues that the ideal of doubt, combined with the demand for strict verification, destroys any possibility of knowing those ideals we hold most dear.[23] In short, both Oakeshott and Polanyi believe that an epistemology that denies the possibility of non-explicit knowledge is the root cause of much that has gone amiss in modern politics

Eric Voegelin

Another twentieth-century thinker whose ideas, at certain points, complement Polanyi's own is Eric Voegelin.[24] Like Polanyi, Voegelin (1901–85) fled Germany to escape the Nazis. This experience helped motivate the concerns and shape the thought of both men. Polanyi and Voegelin both witnessed firsthand the moral and political damage done by those who embraced (whether explicitly or tacitly) a *Weltanschauung* that denied the reality of transcendent moral truth. Both sought to point a way out of the philosophical dead end that had produced the horrors from which they had managed to escape. Voegelin's work reflects a deep and abiding interest in the problem of order. He argues that the political and moral disorder of twentieth-century totalitarianism is rooted in a pathology in the souls of those who have sought to dominate reality rather than to acknowledge human contingency. When human contingency is denied, openness to transcendent reality becomes impossible, for such reality simply cannot be dominated by human will. Recovery, then, is only imaginable when the will to dominate reality is replaced by a recognition of human contingency and a corresponding sense of responsibility to that which transcends human creation.

In a 1948 essay titled "The Origins of Scientism,"[25] Voegelin locates the early signs of scientism in the second half of the sixteenth century, for "it is a movement which accompanied the rise of modern mathematics and physics."[26] According to Voegelin, the impressive gains that were made in the various sciences created a self-assured cast of mind among some of the practitioners of the new science, which led to its over-extension. In other words,

> They began in a fascination with the new sciences to the point of underrating and neglecting the concern to experiences of the spirit; they developed into the assumption that the new science would create a world view that would substitute for the religious order of the soul; and they culminated, in the nineteenth century, in the dictatorial prohibition, on the part of scientistic thinkers, against asking questions of a metaphysical nature.[27]

Voegelin finds three principle features common to all scientistic enterprises:

> (1) the assumption that the mathematized science of natural phenomena is a model science to which all other sciences ought to conform; (2) that all realms of being are accessible to the methods of the sciences of phenomena; and (3) that all reality which is not accessible to sciences of phenomena is either irrelevant or, in the more radical forms of the dogma, illusionary.[28]

Voegelin argues that Newtonian physics—which requires as a postulate the notion of absolute space—combined with the Cartesian materialization of extension, produced a philosophical picture of the universe in which there was no need—indeed, no room—for God.[29] This theoretical removal of God denied the fundamental structure of reality and caused a loss of balance that manifested itself in the political movements of modernity. Indeed, for Voegelin, the "advancement of science and the rationality of politics are interwoven in a social process that, in the perspective of a more distant future, will probably appear as the greatest power orgy in the history of mankind."[30]

The theoretical removal of God—what Voegelin in another work memorably terms "the murder of God"[31]—necessarily places man in a new position of autonomy and self-reliance. Armed with this new freedom from divine control, along with the ontological autonomy that comes with denying the existence of an essential human nature, men committed to scientism are free to attempt to re-create human nature in a manner more suitable than that which had previously been tolerated. In short, scientism frees man to exert his creative passions in order to produce "the man-made being that will succeed the sorry creature of God's making."[32] The political outcome of this attempted reformulation of human nature, however, is quite at odds with utopian visions of peaceful kingdoms, for "historically, the murder of God is not followed by the superman, but by the murder of man."[33] According to Voegelin, the denial of God necessarily produces a false view of reality. This view then manifests itself in political movements that rest on raw power and ultimately result in the massacre of innocents. We must never fall victim to the belief, writes Voegelin, that "an idea is politically unimportant because philosophically it is stark nonsense."[34]

With the modern dominance of scientism, "the spiritual eunuchs," those who denied transcendence, "became the socially effective formers of ideas for the masses."[35] These spiritual eunuchs became the vanguard of the intellectuals, who in turn gave scientism a respectability that was undeserved on purely philosophical terms. This respectability paved the way for increasingly radical endeavors. In Voegelin's words, "without the prestige effect of scientism, such major intellectual scandals as the social success of positivism, or Darwinian evolutionism, or Marxism would be unthinkable."[36]

Scientism seeks to reduce all knowledge to that which can be empirically verified. The realm of facts is assumed to be reducible to scientific terms and therefore objectively knowable, while the realm of values is said to lie outside of scientific methodology and is characterized as merely subjective knowledge. But, as with any theory of knowledge, there are inevitable moral and political implications.

Recall that, according to Polanyi, radical skepticism and a strong impulse toward perfectionism combine to create a volatile political and moral disposition he calls "moral inversion." Radical skepticism denies the reality of moral ideas that serve to limit the means one might legitimately employ in the service of one's ends. But this skepticism is combined with a drive for perfection that pre-Christian skeptics simply did not possess. Thus, moral inversion produces a context in which the most immoral means are employed to secure a vision of political and moral perfection. Of course, the inconsistency of the position is obvious. Nevertheless, Polanyi argues, it is held with a religious intensity that justifies acts that would ordinarily be rejected. Moral inversion, in short, "enables the modern mind, tortured by moral self-doubt, to indulge its moral passions in terms which also satisfy its passion for ruthless objectivity" (PK, 228).

For his part, Voegelin identifies scientism as part of a broader category of noetic pathology (sick consciousness) he terms Gnostic.[37] While Polanyi argues that the moral and political chaos of moral inversion results from an errant view of knowledge, Voegelin argues that Gnosticism is the product of an unbalanced consciousness. Thus, for Polanyi, a proper view of knowledge will open the door to a restoration of balance. For Voegelin, on the other hand, a properly balanced consciousness will, among other things, result in a proper approach to knowing.

Gnostic heresies were the focus of much attention by the early Christian writers. Voegelin defines Gnosticism in a way that only partially overlaps with the theological heresy, and he sees it as an impulse that is very much alive and well. He identifies six general characteristics of Gnosticism. First, the Gnostic is dissatisfied with his situation. Second, the Gnostic believes that this unsatisfactory situation is due to the fact that the world is intrinsically poorly organized. Third, he believes that salvation from this poorly organized world is possible. Fourth, he holds that the order of being will have to be changed. Fifth, this change in the order of being can be produced through human effort. Sixth, this change can only be wrought by those who possess a special knowledge, or gnosis.[38]

Voegelin suggests that the Gnostic is motivated by an all-consuming desire to escape the inherent uncertainty of reality, for the Gnostic craves certainty above all else. Christianity, however, does not offer the certainty he seeks for "uncertainty is the very essence of Christianity."[39] The Christian must walk by faith, which, according to Hebrews 11:1, is the "substance of things hoped for, the evidence of things not seen." "Ontologically," Voegelin submits, " the substance of things hoped for is nowhere to be found but in faith itself; and epistemologically, there is no proof for things unseen but again this very faith."[40] Thus, Gnosticism marks an attempt to circumvent the ontological and epistemological uncertainty of the life of faith through an attempt to alter the fundamental structure of reality. Yet this can only be accomplished by bringing the meaning of existence into the purview of human control: the transcendent truth of reality must be "immanentized."[41]

> The attempt at immanentizing the meaning of existence is fundamentally an attempt at bringing our knowledge of transcendence into a firmer grip than the *cognitio fidei*, the cognition of faith, will afford; and Gnostic experiences offer this firmer grip in so far as they are an expansion of the soul to the point where God is drawn into the existence of man.[42]

While a fear of uncertainty provides the negative impetus to Gnosticism, its positive impetus comes from the "Christian idea of perfection."[43] With God removed from the realm of theoretical possibility, this drive for perfection must be divorced from the transcendent goal of the Christian tradition. The resulting immanentized impulse toward perfectionism, unconstrained by transcendent moral commitments, manifests itself in all manner of inhumane acts.

It is clear that Polanyi's concept of moral inversion overlaps considerably with Voegelin's idea of Gnosticism. Both components

of moral inversion—rational skepticism and moral perfectionism—
find counterparts in Voegelin's account. First, modern skepticism
denies the reality of anything that cannot be empirically verified
and thereby renders the transcendent God of Christianity *a priori*
untenable. Skepticism thoroughly immanentizes reality. Likewise
for Voegelin: a central theme in modern Gnostic movements is the
denial of any transcendent reality. The second element of moral
inversion is perfectionism, an impulse born within the Christian
milieu that finds itself removed from its original context by skepticism. Cut loose from its theological moorings, the perfectionist
impulse directs itself toward refashioning the world unhindered by
transcendent moral restraints. The goal is a new world, one free
from the flaws inherent in the old one, which was corrupted by
superstition and transcendent commitments. The Gnostic opti-
mistically believes that such an effort will produce the certainty for
which he longs—that is, a knowledge perfected as he gains noetic
dominance over reality by an act of sheer will. And because the
aspiration for perfection is unrestrained by moral obligations, both
Gnosticism and moral inversion countenance moral and political
terror as means to their perfect ends.

   Like Polanyi, Voegelin recognizes the importance of faith.
Voegelin looks to Saint Anselm as an example of one who, in the
Augustinian tradition, understood the necessary relationship sym-
bolized in the phrase *fides quaerens intellectum*, "faith in search of
understanding."[44] Voegelin's reflection on the structure of this idea
or symbol "is consciously an expansion of the *fides quaerens intellectum*
beyond Anselm's Christian horizon to the manifold of non- and
pre-Christian theophanic events, as well as to such order as can be

discerned in the revelatory process."[45] Thus, Voegelin looks to this concept for insight into the structure of knowing and extends it from the explicitly Christian field in which it was first articulated into the broader context of non-Christian experience.

According to Voegelin, commentators have consistently misconstrued the intention of Anselm's *Proslogion*, especially Kant, who construed it as an "ontological" argument for the existence of God. These commentators have been so intent on considering whether or not the argument succeeds that "the fides behind the quest has practically faded away."[46] Far from being at its core an argument attempting to prove the existence of God, the *Proslogion* is presented by Anselm in the form of a prayer.[47] Obviously, a prayer presumes the existence of God; thus, it would appear that Anselm is assuming that which he is attempting to prove—a classic case of begging the question. But he is guilty of the fallacy only if the primary function of the *Proslogion* is to demonstrate the existence of God. Voegelin denies this is the case. Instead, "the *Proslogion* is not a treatise about God and his existence, but a prayer of love by the creature to the Creator to grant a more perfect vision of His divinity."[48] This prayer is "a movement of the soul" in which "not Anselm's reason is in quest of understanding but his faith."[49]

The nature of Anselm's quest indicates that "one cannot prove reality by a syllogism; one can only point to it and invite the doubter to look."[50] But such looking implies a degree of trust in the one who points, as well as "a trust in the existence of the unknown structure, a sort of anticipatory knowing of the unknown."[51] Here we see that at the core of true inquiry is a necessary movement of faith, which, far from being replaced once an adequate rational account is achieved, remains an essential ingredient in all true knowing. Thus, "the noetic act, as a *fides quaerens intellectum*, does not destroy the *fides* it tries to understand."[52]

No less that Polanyi, Voegelin's thought is undergirded by a commitment to the view that reality is given and that this reality is normatively structured. While, unlike Polanyi, Voegelin does not attempt to define reality, he frequently employs such phrases as "the structure of reality"[53] and "the order of being"[54] to describe his conception of the nature of reality. For Voegelin, reality is an unchanging fact the structure of which remains a constant regardless of the many ways humans attempt to conceptualize it. It is knowable but ultimately not demonstrable. We achieve deeper insight into the structure of reality by first believing that there is a structure given in reality and that human questing (with divine help) is capable of gaining deeper insight into that reality. The ensuing noetic quest seeks the hidden structure of reality and is motivated by a longing for that which is not yet known.[55] In this way, "contact with reality" is achieved.[56]

Reality is a whole, and humans, being part of that reality, exist within its given structure. This existence is neither one of domination nor pure objectivity, for one cannot dominate that of which one is a part, nor can one separate one's self from the fundamental structure that makes the noetic quest possible. Instead, "man's existence is participation in reality."[57] This participation is neither a particular mode of thought nor an occasional posture, for "participation in being . . . is not a partial involvement of man; he is engaged with the whole of his existence, for participation is existence itself."[58]

For Voegelin, human participation in reality takes place between the divine ground of being and the non-being of death. The divine ground of being is that toward which men ought to strive, for participation in reality "imposes the duty of noetically exploring the structure of reality as far as it is possible and spiritually coping with the insight into its movement from the divine Beginning to the divine Beyond of its structure."[59] A duty noetically to pursue the divine ground of being implies that humans can choose to ignore this duty or deny the divine structure of reality that makes such a duty comprehensible. But such a rejection of the fundamental structure of reality results in the pathology of Gnosticism of which we have already spoken.

Scientism, one of the most prevalent forms of modern Gnosticism, rests on the false assumption that it is possible for the scientist to achieve a completely detached viewpoint from which to observe the facts of his investigation with absolute objectivity. According to scientistic thought, any investigation into the world of facts must necessarily separate itself from the subjective influence of values. Like Polanyi, Voegelin recognizes that this ideal is not only false in practice but necessarily false. It is necessarily false if reality is as Voegelin describes it, for if the human situation is inevitably one of participation, then objective detachment is simply an impossible ideal. Furthermore, despite claims to the contrary, scientists do bring values to bear on their scientific investigations. If scientism operated consistently within its own premises, every fact acquired by means of the prescribed methodology would be considered precisely equal in value. But this is patently not the case, for the very scientist who denies any overt appeal to values inevitably values some methodologically derived facts over oth-ers.[60] This preference, while essential to the work of science, is inexplicable in scientistic terms. According to Voegelin, the fact-value distinction "made sense only if the positivistic dogma was accepted on principle." But such a position could only be accepted by thinkers who had either rejected or ignored classical and Chris-tian philosophy.

> For neither classic nor Christian ethics and politics contain "value-judgments" but elaborate, empirically and critically, the problems of order which derive from philosophical anthro-pology as part of a general ontology. Only when ontology as a science was lost, and when consequently ethics and politics could no longer be understood as sciences of the order in which human nature reaches its maximum actualization, was it pos-sible for this realm of knowledge to become suspect as a field of subjective, uncritical knowledge.[61]

In short, only by rediscovering the science of ontology, with the implied anthropology entailed therein, can the false and ultimately harmful divide between facts and values be overcome. This rediscov-ery of ontology will have at its center a recognition that human exist-ence is a participation in reality, one pole of which is divine.

Alasdair MacIntyre

Alasdair MacIntyre (b. 1929), like Polanyi, has sought to overcome what he perceives to be fatal shortcomings in modern philosophy. Both lament the early-modern rejection of the role of tradition in inquiry. And both believe that the way to move beyond the dead end of modernity is to rediscover the central role played by tradition. They do not necessarily see completely eye-to-eye on these and other matters, but they do share important affinities—affinities MacIntyre has not always been willing to admit. At the very least, both seem to push in the same general direction as they seek an alternative to both Enlightenment rationalism and postmodern nihilism.

Beginning in the late 1970s, MacIntyre started to mention or discuss Polanyi with some frequency.[62] He criticizes him primarily for succumbing to irrationalism—which, according to MacIntyre, was the result of Polanyi's fideism. There is an irony here: not only has MacIntyre himself also been accused of irrationalism,[63] but in his fully developed account of knowledge, he is in agreement with Polanyi on several key points.[64] By the early 1980s, MacIntyre's criticisms of Polanyi seem to have ceased. One might conclude that Polanyi was simply no longer a concern of MacInyre's. But one could also argue that as his thought matured, MacIntyre came to find Polanyi's thought less objectionable.[65] This seems to be evinced in *First Principles, Final Causes and Contemporary Philosophical Issues* (1990), a work in which MacIntyre—who by this time had fully migrated from Marxism to Thomism—makes a positive though fleeting reference to Polanyi. MacIntyre notes that Polayni recognized that, because the virtues form a unified whole, *phronesis* (practical wisdom) requires the possession of the other moral virtues. In this respect, Polanyi's work is anticipated by Aristotle and Aquinas.[66]

In 1977, however, MacIntyre had written that "Polanyi is the Burke of the philosophy of science." MacIntyre did not intend this comparison as a compliment, for he was quite critical of Burke. By linking Polanyi to Burke, he wrote, "all my earlier criticisms of Burke now become relevant to the criticism of Polanyi."[67] Just what are those criticisms? In MacIntyre's words, Burke "wanted to counterpoise tradition and reason and tradition and revolution. Not reason, but prejudice; not revolution, but inherited precedent; these are Burke's key oppositions."[68] MacIntyre repeats the comparison in an article published in 1978:

> Polanyi, of course—like Burke—combined with his emphasis on consensus and tradition a deep commitment to a realistic interpretation of science. Polanyi's realism rested on what he called a "fiduciary commitment." Feyerabend (and less explicitly Kuhn) have retained the fideism; what they have rejected is the realism and with it the objectivism which Polanyi held to as steadfastly as any positivist.[69]

We can perhaps gain a clearer picture of MacIntyre's view of Polanyi by further exploring MacIntyre's critique of Burke.[70]

In *After Virtue*, MacIntyre asserts that Burke contrasted "tradition with reason and the stability of tradition with conflict. Both contrasts obfuscate." In MacIntyre's view, "all reasoning takes place within the context of some traditional mode of thought." Further, traditions in "good order" always "embody continuities of conflict." Thus, "when a tradition becomes Burkean, it is always dying or dead."[71] In *Whose Justice? Which Rationality?* MacIntyre judges that "Burke theorized shoddily" and "was an agent of positive harm."[72] Burke, he continues, "ascribed to traditions in good order, the order as he supposed of following nature, 'wisdom without reflection.' So that no place is left for reflection, rational theorizing as a work of and within tradition."[73] In short, we may summarize MacIntyre's reading of Burke as follows: Burke contrasted tradition and reason. In doing so, he placed stability, consensus, prejudice, and prescription on the side of tradition. On the side of reason, Burke placed conflict, rational reflection, and revolution. But because tradition is separated from any sort of rational reflection, those who favor the alternative of tradition necessarily become fideists, while those who embrace reason may be thought of as rationalists (in the neutral sense of the word). And as we have seen, MacIntyre calls Polanyi the Burke of the philosophy of science.

MacIntyre's understanding of Burke is far from satisfactory, but it concerns us here only to the extent that it involves Polanyi. As we saw in previous chapters, Polanyi does not believe that tradition opposes reason. In his view, all reasoning necessarily occurs within a particular tradition. Second, Polanyi's view of tradition does not imply a commitment to a static view of society; for him, healthy traditions are dynamic. Third, Polanyi does not believe that commitment to a tradition removes all venues for conflict; internal conflict—the ability to rebel against the consensus—is a fundamental element in Polanyi's theory of tradition. All of these positions, in fact, sound very much like MacIntyre's own.

Both MacIntyre and Polanyi point out that a false dilemma has emerged in modern philosophy. On the one hand, the intellectual heirs of Descartes, Bacon, and Locke demand that those things we claim as true must admit of explicit formulation and submit to the requirements of an epistemological method whereby universally valid conclusions can be made with absolute certainty. This is the theory of knowledge that MacIntyre identifies with the "Enlightenment project." Where this approach to knowledge failed to meet its own rigorous demands, both MacIntyre and Polanyi spend considerable effort showing why this was inevitable. They also discuss the reaction against this approach to knowledge. Coming in various forms, the common thread has been a diminished confidence in the attainability of both universality and certainty. Optimistic Enlightenment theories of knowledge—called modern—have largely succumbed to the more pessimistic reactions often categorized as postmodern.[74] Postmodern theories of knowledge are characterized by an emphasis on subjectivity and particularities rather than objectivity and universals. This leads to a dubiety regarding the possibility of achieving anything resembling objective truth or universally valid conclusions. In short, whereas modern theories of knowledge tend enthusiastically to make universal truth claims unsupported by any robust notion of teleology or theology, postmodern theories of knowledge tend toward conclusions that are skeptical and relativistic. Postmodernists generally hold that the particularities of culture, religion, language, and historical era, as well as one's own subjectivity, simply cannot be transcended.

MacIntyre explicitly identifies this dilemma in his *Three Rival Versions of Moral Enquiry*. Here, he correctly recognizes the modern-postmodern dichotomy as a false one. In MacIntyre's idiom, the "encyclopaedists" represent the thinkers of the Enlightenment, while the "genealogists" represent the postmodern reaction against modern epistemic universalism and absolutism.[75] As MacIntyre frames the problem, "*Either* reason is thus impersonal, universal, and disinterested *or* it is the unwitting representative of particular inter-

ests, masking their drive to power by its false pretensions to neutrality and disinterestedness."[76] But, as MacIntyre points out, there
is a third alternative, one he dubs "tradition." He describes it as
follows:

> What this [false] alternative conceals from view is a third possi-
> bility, the possibility that reason can only move towards being
> genuinely universal and impersonal insofar as it is neither neu-
> tral nor disinterested, that membership in a particular type of
> moral community, one from which fundamental dissent has to
> be excluded, is a condition for genuinely rational enquiry and
> more especially for moral and theological enquiry. . . . A prior
> commitment is required and the conclusions which emerge as
> enquiry progresses will of course have been partially and cru-
> cially predetermined by the nature of this initial commitment.[77]

This summary brings together many of the elements we have
discussed so far. The impersonal and universalistic ideals of Enlightenment theories of knowledge must be rejected, but such
rejection does not necessarily imply that postmodern relativism
wins by default. The Enlightenment rationalist sought to reject all
dependence on tradition in an attempt to secure direct and
unmediated access to universal and timeless truth. MacIntyre, by
contrast, recognizes that rationality is tradition-dependent. But
he denies that this fact of human existence is fatal to any idea of
truth that transcends particularity. Concepts like authority, submission, and tradition—all of which are rejected by Enlightenment rationalists—are embraced by MacIntyre as necessary for
human knowing. His tradition-constituted theory of knowledge is

rescued from postmodern skepticism and relativism by his underlying commitment to realism, which affirms the existence of an external reality that is both timeless and knowable. Since humans cannot completely transcend the particularities of our personal situations, our knowledge of reality will always be colored by the particularities in which we live; these serve as the lens through which we view reality. But despite the imperfect nature of our knowing, it is still properly conceived as knowing. While this account provides far less certainty than the Enlightenment rationalist hoped, it is far more substantive than that for which the postmodernist has settled.

Thus, the apparent dichotomy between what Polanyi calls "objectivism" and "nihilism" and what MacIntyre calls the "encyclopaedists" and the "genealogists" actually represents an inevitable progression. In order to extricate ourselves from the terminal end of this downward spiral, we must "restore the balance" of our thought by recognizing that knowing requires personal participation in the form of commitment. Because knowing is a skill, we must submit ourselves to the authority of a tradition and of those who have already become masters. When we acknowledge the fiduciary nature of all knowing, the barrier that was erected between facts and values collapses. The humanities can once again be admitted as legitimate objects of knowledge. A commitment to the existence of an independent reality—one with which we can make contact—holds this account together, as does the responsibility to embrace our conclusions with universal intent. This being the case, our freedom to act is tempered by our responsibility to conform to reality as we find it (PK, 309). Polanyi describes the dilemma and his solution to it as follows:

Objectivism seeks to relieve us from all responsibility for the holding of our beliefs. That is why it can be logically expanded to systems of thought in which the responsibility of the human person is eliminated from the life and society of man. In recoiling from objectivism, we would acquire a nihilistic freedom of action but for the fact that our protest is made in the name of higher allegiances. We cast off the limitations of objectivism in order to fulfil our calling, which bids us to make up our minds about the whole range of matters with which man is properly concerned (PK, 323–24).

Thus, freedom from objectivism does not necessarily imply a retreat into nihilism. On the contrary, rather than being the opposite of objectivism, nihilism is objectivism's logical end. By affirming the personal element in knowing, we regain the capacity to affirm ideals that we know to be true but cannot prove scientifically. In doing so, we commit ourselves to pursuing those ideals responsibly, and we do so in service of the reality with which we strive to make contact.

Polanyi and MacIntyre both recognize that their respective approaches to recovering that which has been lost entail a renewed possibility for meaningful moral and theological discussion. MacIntyre argues that teleology and realism seem to be inherently theistic; therefore, to embrace a coherent account that includes teleology and realism is simultaneously to embrace its underlying theism.[78] Polanyi, too, recognizes that his alternative to the blind alley of philosophical modernity opens the door to theism. In the concluding paragraphs of his *Science, Faith and Society,* he writes of the "transcendent obligations" a moral society ought to pursue.

The well-being of society, he argues, is secondary to the fulfillment of these obligations in "the spiritual field." But such notions "would seem to call for an extension in the direction towards God." The book ends on a hopeful note: "[M]odern man will eventually return to God through the clarification of his cultural and social purposes. Knowledge of reality and the acceptance of obligations which guide our consciences, once firmly realized, will reveal to us God in man and society" (SFS, 83–84).[79]

Polanyi's Legacy

The modern world, mired in what Polanyi called "objectivist" methods of thought, finds itself plagued by maladies that bear the unique stamp of the assumptions which undergird modernity. In terms of religion and ethics, deep skepticism about the reality of transcendent truth—or at least about the human capacity to know such truth—characterizes much of the modern disposition. Philosophical naturalism and its attendant materialism have truncated the scope of human concern, if not the horizon of human possibility. Modern optimism has gradually given way to postmodern despair— or at best, to the resignation that accompanies the acceptance of intellectual limitation and spiritual isolation. This coarsening of spiritual sensibilities has brought with it the inability to distinguish the sacred from the profane, the noble from the ignoble, that which deserves to be preserved from that which can be carelessly discarded.

Philosophical materialism, when injected into an industrialized society, manifests itself socially in another form of materialism—namely, consumerism. While all living creatures are necessarily consumers, consumerism as such is something altogether new. Industrialization provides the mass production necessary to sustain a society of individuals dedicated primarily to the acquisition of material goods, while philosophical materialism provides the psychological and spiritual license for this headlong, subhuman pursuit. In such a milieu, fidelity to one's home or community is eroded by the primary value of acquisition. Thus, we see modern consumers embracing a relentlessly mobile existence, trading ties with extended family and community for the promise of a bigger paycheck or, more generally, an improved "quality of life." which is almost always reducible to material terms (or more broadly hedonistic ones, which is merely an instance of the commodification of pleasure). In short, modern man is characterized in large part by a skepticism that manifests itself in both consumerism and rootlessness. And as the scope of human concerns has narrowed and lowered, the social commitments and priorities necessary for the sustenance of healthy communities have been largely jettisoned. Thus, as human concerns constrict to the single (though infinitely variegated) moment of the consumer, the social and political ties that provide the necessary ballast for a fully human existence are violently rent. When the acquisition of material goods or hedonistic satisfaction becomes the engine of desire, although we may still utter words of fidelity to parent, sibling, or community, those attachments will always find themselves in second place to the more urgent and tangible. Modern rootlessness is, at least in part, a function of skepticism concerning the sacred nature of one's family or home, which are reduced merely to accretions we must, often with considerable pain, scrape away as we pursue that for which our hearts truly long.

But it is not only the materialism born of skepticism that produces modern nomads. The demands of objectivism itself condition the modern mind to think in terms of placeless places, or, in Thomas Nagel's words, purport to give us a "view from nowhere." When such a stance is offered as an ideal, any fidelity to a particular place or a particular set of assumptions grounded in local tradition and prejudice will be seen as a barrier that inhibits an accurate perception of reality. Objectivism, in short, reiterates the longing of Descartes, who sought an Archimedean point—a point outside all reality—upon which to stake his epistemological fortunes.

Of course, if there is no possibility of the sacred, that is, if all notions of transcendent truth are dissolved in the cauldron of skepticism, morality is necessarily reduced to some form of utilitarian calculus. But utilitarianism is ill-equipped to provide the binding force necessary to sustain communities. The sorts of commitments that a common religion—or, more broadly, a common good—engender cannot be sustained in the thin atmosphere of the greatest-happiness principle.

Robust community life of the sort that best encourages and sustains human flourishing requires some real good that transcends individual or corporate pleasure. The loss of community so often lamented in our day, the decline of social capital, the image of the solitary bowler, have emerged hand-in-hand with the phenomena of consumerism. That these conditions share the same historical and social context is initially surprising. After all, it would seem that an increase in material goods should make us better equipped to engage our neighbors and actively to participate in the lives of our communities. But where the material means may be available, the spiritual urge seems to diminish inversely. All too often, the modern person finds himself barricaded behind a mountain of material goods and lacking the desire to extend himself beyond the confines of a narrow circle of friends and family.

We have at this point broached a broad array of social and political issues that seem traceable to a skeptical impulse. This impulse, in turn, is located in the prejudices and mental habits of objectivism. And while Polanyi shows how objectivism served to justify the political excesses of the twentieth century, the passion of that impulse seems to have cooled since Polanyi's time. Today, skepticism remains intact, but perfectionism has been replaced by the gentler impulse of hedonism. This phenomenon is reflected in the avalanche of self-help books and programs promising to maximize individual potential (which translates directly into personal fulfillment, a euphemism for pleasure). This same hedonist impulse at least in part manifests itself in the determined effort to globalize markets, for more consumers means more profits, which in turn makes possible the sustenance of our own material desires. Politically, this policy of open global markets and the peace that trade requires is best facilitated within an international community consisting of liberal democracies. But here, we do well to recall Polanyi's words: liberty must ultimately be in service, not of trade, but of transcendent ideals. A totally secularized conception of political liberty would, it seems, be unable to perpetuate its own freedom. Liberty can only operate within the boundaries recognized and respected as originating beyond human will.

Does Polanyi help extricate us from the modern/postmodern conundrum? Can his understanding of knowing point out a third way by which to transcend the failures of the modern project without stumbling into the quagmire of postmodern skepticism? Does Polanyi give us the resources to overcome the rootless skepticism that lies at the heart of modern consumerism and the breakdown of richly textured human communities? Polanyi harbors no romantic belief that the modern world can simply return to a premodern understanding of truth. At the same time, he recognizes that the moral and political excesses of the twentieth century were rooted in the fact that modern conceptions of knowledge prevent us from making truth claims about the very things we once held, and perhaps still do hold, most dear. The question is whether we can recover the capacity to speak meaningfully of truths that do not admit of explicit, empirical justification—truths of a moral and spiritual sort. The postmodernist would have us speak of preferences derived from individual communities, but this only suggests a relativism of communities. Such a relativism, when those preferences come into conflict, can ultimately only be resolved by force. In this context, truth is at root not more than whatever the most powerful community says it is. Truth, in this sense, loses any independent ontological status; it resides in the will of individuals and communities rather than in reality itself.

Polanyi, as we have seen, affirms as a central tenet of his position the independent existence of reality. Human knowers can make contact with this reality, although their knowledge of it is never complete or exhaustive. Precisely the same belief drives the scientist to pursue a problem. He believes that a solution exists, and this belief spurs him on in his relentless pursuit of the prize. Polanyi well understood the passion for discovery that motivates the scientist. The satisfaction derived from his pursuit of that passion is the product of a deepening sense of coherence, as when a puzzle piece makes a picture come into view or a turn of the key brings a lock's tumblers into place. At that moment, there is no doubt in the scientist's mind that the solution is correct; although, more often than not, the discoverer does not recognize the full implications of what he has discovered. Though he makes contact with reality in discerning it, his discovery is freighted with indeterminate future manifestations. But these latent possibilities, perhaps not even imagined by the discoverer, drive the next generation in an ongoing quest to understand the reality for which we all strive. Once the artificial divide between facts and values is put aside, we can recognize that this same process of discovery applies not only to the sciences, but to such humane endeavors as morality, aesthetics, and religion as well.

Polanyi's theory of tacit knowing acknowledges the central role of faith. This emphasis on faith opens the door to a reintroduction of the transcendent. For Polanyi, knowing necessarily entails the integration of subsidiary elements into a focal whole through the active participation of the knower. While the process of tacit knowing does not depend on any explicitly religious or theological presuppositions, Polanyi is quick to point out that his theory of knowledge, by giving credence to beliefs that are not empirically verifiable, provides a way to reclaim religious, moral, and aesthetic belief. We must recognize the fiduciary framework of all knowledge, and in so doing, overcome the prejudice produced by our modern commitment to objectivism. This shift in self-understanding will reestablish the contingent and dependent nature of human thought. Ultimately, it will point to a truth that transcends human cognition.

Contrary to the objectivist demand for a purely objective and universal conception of knowledge, Polanyi's conception of knowing tutors the mind to recognize that human beings are necessarily and unavoidably rooted in a particular place. The from-to structure of all knowing requires that we acknowledge that all attempts to grasp reality necessarily begin *from* some place. The subsidiaries we hold as we focus upon the object of our attention are rooted in the places that we inhabit both physically and mentally. When Polanyi argues that the body is an essential component in knowing the world around us, he necessarily implies that we must acknowledge that the body is *some place*—a place that has particular physical characteristics, a particular culture, a particular language, and particular habits, customs, and mores. There is no view from nowhere.

This insight was lost under the attack of the philosophical ideas that emerged in the early-modern period. Although it must be regained, such recovery is no easy task, for today, objectivist habits of mind have worked their way into the very manner in which we live. Philosophical rootlessness has produced geographic rootlessness, and to reverse the habit of geographic rootlessness, we must go to the source of the problem and retool our philosophical assumptions.

This is where Polanyi's thought is crucial. Recognizing that, by taking an epistemological wrong turn, we have become lost, he reintroduces the personal participation of the knower into the process of knowing. As a result, the human knower finds himself reconnected to the world; he is no longer off stage, looking in at a scene in which he is playing a part. Polanyi's theory of tacit knowing provides the knower with an intuitively satisfying account that does not leave him out of the equation. The knower, once again, becomes a central and active participant engaged in the pursuit of truth.

The Cartesian dream of purely objective knowledge is an illusion. That kind of pristinely impersonal viewpoint is an unattainable ideal, yet there is an option other than a retreat into skepticism: the idea of personal knowledge. Buoyed by this understanding, human knowers can embrace the responsibility to make contact with a hidden but knowable reality.

A complete and full comprehension of reality will never be achieved, but the fact that we can truly make contact with reality provides the impetus for our continued pursuit of understanding. And because reality comprises more than matter, it is not reducible merely to the laws of physics and chemistry. Polanyi stakes out his position in opposition to those whose view is truncated by false conceptions of both the nature of knowing and the nature of reality. With his insistence that faith necessarily underlies the human experience, that knowing is essentially personal and requires the responsible action of individual knowers, and that the most real entities are not tangible, Polanyi points a way out of the dark forest of rational skepticism and systematic doubt. He shows us how we might once again speak meaningfully of the good, the true, and the beautiful. And he shows us how we might recover an understanding of the importance of the places we inhabit and the persons with whom we live.

NOTES

Preface

1. W. B. Yeats, "The Second Coming," in "The Poems of W. B. Yeats" ed. Richard J. Finneran. (New York: MacMillan Publishing Company, 1983): 187.
2. T. S. Eliot, "Choruses from 'The Rock,'" The Complete Poems and Plays, 1909–1950 (New York: Harcourt, Brace & World, 1971): 96.

Chapter One

1. William Taussig Scott and Martin X. Moleski, S.J., *Michael Polanyi: Scientist and Philosopher* (New York: Oxford University Press, 2005), 8.
2. Michael Polanyi Papers [Box 38, Folder 8], Special Collection Research Center, University of Chicago Library.
3. Paul Ignotus, "The Hungary of Michael Polanyi," published in *The Logic of Personal Knowledge: Essays Presented to Michael Polanyi on his Seventieth Birthday, 11th March 1961* (London: Routledge & Kegan Paul), 12.
4. Michael Polanyi Papers, Box 38, Folder 8, Special Collection Research Center, University of Chicago Library.
5. Ibid.
6. Ibid.
7. Scott and Moleski, *Michael Polanyi,* 45.
8. Drusilla Scott, *Everyman Revived: The Common Sense of Michael Polanyi*

(Grand Rapids, MI: William B. Eerdmans Publishing Co., 1985), 182, and Scott and Moleski, 194.

9. Scott and Moleski, *Michael Polanyi,* 57.

10. William Taussig Scott, "At the Wheel of the World: The Life and Times of Michael Polanyi," *Tradition & Discovery* 25, no. 3 (1998–99), 18.

11. Scott and Moleski, *Michael Polanyi,* 85.

12. Letter from Polanyi to Arthur Lapworth, March 15, 1932 (German). See Michael Polanyi Papers, Box 2, Folder 8.

13. Scott and Moleski, *Michael Polanyi,* 161.

14. Ibid., 193.

15. Michael Polanyi Papers, Box 5, Folder 4.

16. Ibid.

17. E. P. Wigner and R. A. Hodgkin, "Biographical Memoirs of Fellows of the Royal Society," Vol. 23, Nov.–Dec. (1977), 425.

18. Wigner and Hodgkin, *Michael Polanyi,* 426

19. Scott and Moleski, *Michael Polanyi,* 208.

20. Wigner and Hodgkin, *Michael Polanyi,* 426.

21. Scott and Moleski, *Michael Polanyi,* 277.

22. Michael Polanyi Papers, Box 38, Folder 8.

23. Michael Polanyi Papers, Box 6, Folder 9.

Chapter Two

1. Polanyi first uses this term in print in 1948 ("The Span of Central Direction," republished in LL). Hayek's first published use of the term occurs in his 1960 work, *The Constitution of Liberty* (Chicago: University of Chicago Press, 1960). Hayek acknowledges his debt to Polanyi on page 160.

2. Scott and Moleski, *Michael Polanyi,* 167–68.

3. Letter from Polanyi to Karl Mannheim, April 19, 1944. Michael Polanyi Papers, Box 4, Folder 11.

4. Paul Craig Roberts and Norman Van Cott, "Polanyi's Economics," *Tradition & Discovery* 25, no. 3 (1998–99), 26.

5. Ibid., 26.

6. Ibid., 26.

7. Wigner and Hodgkin, "Biographical Memoirs," 424.

8. Paul Ignotus, "The Hungary of Michael Polanyi," in *The Logic of Personal Knowledge,* 11.

9. Karl Polanyi, *The Great Transformation* (Boston: Beacon Press, 2001), 3–4.

10. Ibid., 60.

11. Ibid., 171.

12. Ibid., 187.

13. Ibid., 75.

14. Ibid., 141.

15. Ibid., 242.

16. Ibid., 258.

17. Ibid., 255.

18. Ibid., 259.

19. Ibid., 268.

20. Letter from Karl Polanyi, January 17, 1936, Michael Polanyi Papers, Box 17, Folder 6.

21. Letter from Karl Polanyi, November 1, 1945, Michael Polanyi Papers, Box 17, Folder 11.

22. Polanyi uses the terms "faith" and "belief" interchangeably.

23. "Throughout the formative centuries of modern science, the rejection of authority was its battle-cry" (KB, 65).

24. Arthur Koestler, *Darkness at Noon*, trans. Daphne Hardy (New York: Bantam Books, 1966), 149.

25. Polanyi refers to Popper's emphasis on falsifiability as a contemporary example of the objectivist ideal of a dispassionate pursuit of knowledge. "There is indeed an idealization of this [dispassionate nature of science] current today, which deems the scientist not only indifferent to the outcome of his surmises, but actually seeking their refutation. This is not only contrary to experience, but logically inconceivable. The surmises of a working scientist are *born of the imagination seeking discovery*. Such effort *risks* defeat but never *seeks* it; it is in fact his craving for success that makes the scientist take the risk of failure. There is no other way. Courts of law employ two separate lawyers to argue opposite pleas, because it is only by a passionate commitment to a particular view that the imagination can discover the evidence that supports it" (TD, 78–79; M, 195).

26. John Henry Newman, *The Idea of a University* (Notre Dame, IN: University of Notre Dame Press, 1982). See especially Part 1, Discourse 5: "Knowledge for its own End."

27. T. S. Eliot, *The Sacred Wood* (London: Faber & Faber, 1997).

28. Letter from T.S. Eliot, March 5, 1945, Michael Polanyi Papers, Box 4, Folder 12.

29. Harry Prosch, "Polanyi's Ethics," *Ethics* 82 (1972), 91.

30. KB, 65; SEP, 215; TD, 63; LL, 10, 18.
31. Cf. KB, 8, 65.
32. Cf. TD, 57; 85.
33. Cf. KB, 67–69; LL, 121–22.

Chapter Three

1. Polanyi translates the Latin: "Unless ye believe, ye shall not understand." At other points, Polanyi employs a similar Latin phrase, *fides quaerens intellectum*, which translates as "to believe in order to know" (SFS, 15; cf. SFS, 45; TD, 61).
2. Cf. FR, 237–39.
3. "And I think that today we can feel the balance of mental needs tilting back once again" (SFS, 27).
4. Cf. PK, 31.
5. Francis Bacon, *Novum Organum*, CXXX.
6. Polanyi notes that the word "uncritically" is more precisely rendered as "a-critically" (PK, 264 n.2; SM, 17).
7. Cf. SFS, 64, 81.
8. Cf. PK, vii.
9. Cf. SM, 28–29.
10. Cf. LP, 30.
11. Ibid.
12. Polanyi's recognition that the body plays a necessary and indispensable part in the knowing process represents an important confluence with the work of Maurice Merleau-Ponty. See Merleau-Ponty's *Phenomenology of Perception*, trans. Colin Smith (New York: Routledge & Kegan Paul, 1962). The original French version was published in 1945. Marjorie Grene, in her book *The Knower and the Known* (New York: Basic Books, 1966), points out the important similarities between these two thinkers.
13. Cf. SM, 18.
14. See Plato, *Meno*, 80d–e.
15. Cf. SFS, 34.
16. Cf. CI, 117.
17. There is an ongoing discussion among Polanyi scholars regarding the nature of Polanyi's realism. See, for example, *Tradition & Discovery* 26, no. 3 (1999–2000). The entire issue is dedicated to exploring this topic.
18. Aristotle of course also makes this point. See *Politics*, 1253a 8–18. Humans, unlike other animals, possess *logos*, the power of rational discourse.

19. Cf. PK, 80.
20. In 1966, Polanyi sent a copy of his article "Sense-Giving and Sense-Receiv-ing" to linguist Noam Chomsky. In that article, Polanyi mentions Chomsky several times and suggests the manner in which his theory of tacit knowing substantiates Chomsky's account of generative grammar. Chomsky was, by that time, well aware of Polanyi's work. He wrote to thank Polanyi for the essay and continued: "I have been following your work very closely for years, and have found it to be a constant source of great stimulation and insight. . . . I feel that we are working along rather parallel lines." Letter from Noam Chomsky, November 6, 1966, Michael Polanyi Papers, Box 6, Folder 8.
21. Cf. PK, 266–67; 318–19; SFS, 83.
22. Cf. PK, 313.
23. Cf. Thomas Kuhn on "gestalt switch" in *The Structure of Scientific Revolutions,* 3rd ed. (Chicago: University of Chicago Press, 1962).
24. "As Saint Augustine viewed it, a religious belief cannot be achieved by our deliberate efforts and choice. It is a gift of God and may remain inexplicably denied to some of us" (M, 180). See also SFS, 67; PK, 324.
25. Cf. PK, 403.
26. Cf. TD, 77–78.
27. David Hume most famously pointed out the problem of moving from facts to values: "In every system of morality, which I have hitherto met with, I have always remarked, that the author proceeds for some time in the ordinary way of reasoning, and establishes the being of a God, or makes observations concerning human affairs; when of a sudden I am surprised to find, that instead of the usual copulations of propositions, *is,* and *is not,* I meet with no proposition that is not connected with an *ought,* or an *ought not.* This change is imperceptible; but is, however, of the last consequence. For as this *ought,* or *ought not,* expresses some new relation or affirmation, it is necessary that it should be observed and explained; and at the same time that a reason should be given, for what seems altogether inconceivable, how this new relation can be a deduction from others, which are entirely different from it" David Hume, *A Treatise of Human Nature* (1740), Book III, Part I, sec. 1.
28. Cf. PK, 133–34, 249.
29. Polanyi writes: "The great movement for independent thought instilled in the modern mind a desperate refusal of all knowledge that is not absolutely impersonal, and this implied in its turn a mechanical conception of man which was bound to deny man's capacity for independent thought" (PK, 214).

30. See chapter 4, note 2.
31. "I accept the responsibility for drawing an ever indeterminate knowledge from unspecifiable clues, with an aim to universal validity; and this belief includes the acknowledgment of other persons as responsible centres of equally unspecifiable operations, aiming likewise at universal validity" (PK, 336).
32. Cf. PK, 316; SFS, 70, 71, 73.
33. PK, 109, 145, 214, 306.
34. Thomas Kuhn, author of the influential *Structure of Scientific Revolutions*, acknowledges his debt to Polanyi in a footnote (44). In 1961, at Kuhn's invitation, Polanyi served as a commentator on a paper by Kuhn. Kuhn had heard Polanyi speak at Stanford in 1958 and was familiar with his work. Polanyi began by observing that "the paper by Mr. Thomas Kuhn may arouse opposition from various quarters but not from me." As Scott and Moleski put it, Polanyi "agreed with Kuhn's statement that research is dependent on a deep commitment to established beliefs. However, Polanyi did not accept Kuhn's simple dichotomy between normal science conducted within a standard paradigm and revolutionary science that creates new paradigms because remarkable advances have been made just by taking current paradigms seriously" (Scott and Moleski, *Michael Polanyi*, 246). Kuhn and Polanyi further part company on the issue of realism. This makes Kuhn vulnerable to accusations of relativism in a way that Polanyi is not. In a postscript to the third edition of his book, Kuhn attempts to clarify his position. "A scientific theory is usually felt to be better than its predecessors not only in the sense that it is a better instrument for discovering and solving puzzles but also because it is somehow a better representation of what nature is really like. One often hears that successive theories grow ever closer to, or approximate more and more closely to, the truth. Apparently generalizations like that refer not to the puzzle-solutions and the concrete predictions derived from a theory but rather to its ontology, to the match, that is, between the entities with which the theory populates nature and what is 'really there.' Perhaps there is some other way of salvaging the notion of 'truth' for application to whole-theories, but this one will not do" (206). In short, where Polanyi's thought rests on the belief that human knowers can make contact with reality, Kuhn denies that this ontological claim has any meaning.
35. According to Scott and Moleski, "the decisive point that brought him into

very close relationship with the Pauline scheme of redemption was the reading of Reinhold Niebuhr's two-volume work *The Nature and Destiny of Man*" (262).

Chapter Four

1. In *Science, Faith, and Society*, Polanyi refers to these as part of a "spiritual reality." In the 1964 republication of that work, he notes in a new introduction that he has come to "prefer to call it a belief in the reality of emergent meaning and truth" (SFS, 17).

2. Polanyi scholars disagree concerning Polanyi's view of the status of moral, religious, and artistic reality. On the one hand, there are those, like me, who argue that a central theme of Polanyi's thought is showing how all fields of inquiry are essentially the same in epistemological terms. On the other hand, there are those (represented by thinkers such as Harry Prosch, who collaborated with Polanyi in his last book, *Meaning*) who argue that Polanyi maintained a distinction between scientific reality, which is independent of the knower, and moral, religious, and artistic reality, which is ontologically dependent upon the creative imagination of the human knower. For examples of the first position, see Richard Gelwick, *The Way of Discovery: An Introduction to the Thought of Michael Polanyi* (New York: Oxford University Press, 1977); Maben Walter Poirier, "Harry Prosch's Modernism," *Tradition & Discovery* 16, no. 2 (1998), 32–39. For examples of the second approach, see Harry Prosch's response to Gelwick in *Ethics* 89 (1979), 211–16. See also his response to Poirier in "Those Missing 'Objects,'" *Tradition & Discovery* 17, nos. 1–2 (1990), 17–20; Harry Prosch, *Michael Polanyi: A Critical Exposition* (Albany, NY: State University of New York Press, 1986), especially chapters 17 and 18; and Harry Prosch, "Polanyi's Ethics," *Ethics* 82 (1972), 91–113. In addition, see *Zygon* 17 (1982), an issue which focuses on Polanyi's thought. This topic comes up with some regularity in the journal *Tradition & Discovery*. See, for example, the issue on Polanyi's realism, 26, no. 3 (1999–2000).

3. Scott and Moleski, *Michael Polanyi*, 213.

4. Ibid., 197.

5. Scott, *Everyman Revived*, 182.

6. Letter from Polanyi to J. H. Oldham, Aug. 16, 1964, Michael Polanyi Papers, Box 15, Folder 5.

7. Thomas F. Torrance, "Michael Polanyi and the Christian Faith—A Personal Report," *Tradition & Discovery*, 27, no. 2 (2000–2001), 30.

8. See, for example, Thomas Torrance, *Belief in Science and in Christian Life: The Relevance of Michael Polanyi's Thought for Christian Faith and Life* (Edinburgh: Handsel Press, 1980); and his *Reality and Scientific Theology* (Edinburgh: Scottish Academic Press, 1985).

9. Leslie Newbigin, *The Gospel in a Pluralist Society* (Grand Rapids, MI: William B. Eerdmans Publishing Co., 1989).

10. Terence Kennedy, *The Morality of Knowledge* (Rome, 1979). Quoted in Prosch, *Michael Polanyi*, 256.

11. Torrance, "Michael Polanyi and the Christian Faith," 29–31.

12. Scott, *Everyman Revived*, 181–82.

13. Letter from J. H. Oldham to Polanyi, Sept. 8,1947, Michael Polanyi Papers, Box 15, Folder 3.

14. Letter from J. H. Oldham to Polanyi, May 13, 1948, Michael Polanyi Papers, Box 15, Folder 4.

15. Letter from Polanyi to J. H. Oldham, May 31, 1948, Michael Polanyi Papers, Box 15, Folder 4.

16. Quoted in Scott, *Everyman Revived*, 182–83.

17. Torrance, "Michael Polanyi and the Christian Faith," 30.

18. C. S. Lewis, "Meditation in a Toolshed," in Walter Hooper, ed., *God in the Dock* (Grand Rapids, MI: William B. Eerdmans Publishing Co., 1970), 212–15.

19. See David Hume, *An Enquiry Concerning Human Understanding*, section X.

20. Stephen Jay Gould, *Rocks of Ages* (New York: Ballantine Books, 1999).

21. In his personal notes, Polanyi reiterates this point and argues that science itself cannot live up to its own ideals: "Mr. [Rom] Harré recommended that we recognize that judged by scientific standards, religion is simply false. He would offer to religion immunity from all questions of fact. But on what justification? Occam and later Locke suggested something similar, but it has long since lost its hold on modern thought.

    "We must start instead from the fact that the observational standards proclaimed by science would—if strictly applied—deprive science itself of its foundations. This is where we must begin. Science itself is in danger of these impossible standards." Michael Polanyi Papers, Box 22, Folder 6.

22. It is interesting to note that advocates of the so-called Intelligent Design critique of neo-Darwinism occasionally mention Polanyi's critique of mate-

rialism as an important forerunner of their position. Of course, Polanyi, unlike many in the Intelligent Design movement, never repudiated evolution per se, but he was very critical of any purely materialistic account of human origins or knowledge.

Chapter Five

1. Letter from William F. Buckley, August 4,1964, Michael Polanyi Papers, Box 6, Folder 6.
2. Letter from Polanyi to William F. Buckley, March 21, 1968, Michael Polanyi Papers, Box 6, Folder 12.
3. Letter from Edward Shils, June 4, 1957, Michael Polanyi Papers, Box 5, Folder 10.
4. Letter from Polanyi to Daniel Patrick Moynihan, June 12, 1969, Michael Polanyi Papers, Box 7, Folder 13.
5. Letter from Polayni to Daniel Patrick Moynihan, April 13, 1970, Michael Polanyi Papers, Box 8, Folder 8.
6. Letter from Daniel Patrick Moynihan, July 2, 1970, Michael Polanyi Papers, Box 8, Folder 12.
7. Michael Oakeshott, "The Human Coefficient," *Encounter* 11 (1958), 77–80.
8. Ibid., 77. While this seems primarily a stylistic point, Oakeshott, who held that the purpose of philosophy is clearly to define all pertinent concepts, found Polanyi's work substantively problematic as well. Cf. Marjorie Grene's comments on the relationship between Polanyi's style and his philosophical project in "'Tacit Knowing' Grounds for a Revolution in Philosophy," *Journal of the British Society for Phenomenology* 8, no. 3 (1977), 167–68.
9. Oakeshott, "The Human Coefficient," 79.
10. Michael Oakeshott, *Rationalism in Politics* (Indianapolis, IN: Liberty Fund, 1991), 44.
11. Oakeshott, "The Human Coefficient," 79.
12. Ibid.
13. Michael Oakeshott, "John Locke," *Cambridge Review* 54 (1932–33), 72.
14. A key difference between idealism and realism is their different standards for verifying truth. For the idealist, coherence is the sole criterion; for Polanyi, the realist, truth consists in making contact with an external reality.
15. Oakeshott, *Rationalism in Politics*, 12.
16. Ibid.

17. Ibid., 13, n4.

18. Michael Oakeshott, "Science and Society," *Cambridge Journal* 1 (1947–48), 692, n1.

19. It should be pointed out that, in the two footnotes where Oakeshott refers to the parallels between his concepts of practical and technical knowledge and Polanyi's discussion of similar concepts, he refers exclusively to *Science, Faith and Society*. In that early work, Polanyi had not yet developed his theory of tacit knowing, with its distinction between focal and subsidiary elements. Thus, while Oakeshott is quite correct to see the similarities between his work and Polanyi's at this stage, Polanyi later develops this area much more thoroughly than Oakeshott does. Thus, Polanyi's later work significantly supercedes Oakeshott's conception of technical and practical knowledge by virtue of its more complex development.

20. See Oakeshott, "Rationalism in Politics" in *Rationalism in Politics*, 35–42, and Polanyi, SFS.

21. PK, vii, 3, 264–68, 269–98, 381.

22. Oakeshott, *Rationalism in Politics*, 15.

23. PK, 269–98.

24. Although, as far as I can tell, neither Polanyi nor Voegelin ever cites the other, they were at least minimally familiar with each other and met at on at least one occasion. In 1960, Raymond Aron edited a collection of essays on the topic of technology. The conference that had spawned this collection included twenty-one scholars from a wide variety of disciplines. Among the participants were such notables as Bertrand de Jouvenel and Robert Oppenheimer as well as Michael Polanyi and Eric Voegelin. Voegelin presented a paper titled "Industrial Society in Search of Reason." The English translation of Aron's volume was published in 1963 as *World Technology and Human Destiny*, ed. Raymond Aron (Ann Arbor, MI: University of Michigan Press, 1963).

25. Eric Voegelin, "The Origins of Scientism," *Social Research* 15 (1948), 462–94.

26. Ibid., 462.

27. Ibid.

28. Ibid. See also Eric Voegelin, *The New Science of Politics*, (Chicago: University of Chicago Press, 1952), 4.

29. Voegelin, "The Origins of Scientism," 472.

30. Ibid., 486.

31. Eric Voegelin, *Science, Politics and Gnosticism* (Washington, DC: Regnery Publishing Inc., 1968), 35–50.

32. Voegelin, "The Origins of Scientism," 488.
33. Voegelin, *Science, Politics and Gnosticism*, 43.
34. Voegelin, "The Origins of Scientism," 487.
35. Ibid., 494.
36. Ibid., 493.
37. Voegelin notes that scientism is "one of the strongest Gnostic movements in Western society" (*The New Science of Politics*, 127).
38. Voegelin, *Science, Politics and Gnosticism*, 59–60.
39. Voegelin, *The New Science of Politics*, 122.
40. Ibid.
41. See Eric Voegelin, *The Ecumenic Age, Vol. 4, Order and History* (Baton Rouge, LA: Louisiana State University Press, 1974), 18–28.
42. Voegelin, *The New Science of Politics*, 124.
43. Voegelin, *Science, Politics and Gnosticism*, 61.
44. Polanyi, too, emphasizes the importance of this concept and invokes the same phrase. Cf. SFS, 15, 45; PK, 266; TD, 61.
45. Eric Voegelin, "The Beginning and the Beyond: A Meditation on Truth," *The Collected Works of Eric Voegelin*, vol. 28, ed. Thomas A. Hollweck and Paul Caringella (Baton Rouge, LA: Louisiana State University Press, 1989): 173–232; Voegelin, "The Beginning and the Beyond," 191.
46. Voegelin, "The Beginning and the Beyond," 192.
47. Ibid. 193. Alasdair MacIntyre, too, makes this point. "Anselm's arguments are in no way accidentally in the form of prayer. To understand the required concept adequately the mind must already be directed by faith toward its true perfection. The rational justification of belief in the object of faith is internal to the life of faith" (*Three Rival Versions of Moral Enquiry*, Notre Dame, IN: University of Notre Dame Press, 1990), 95–96.
48. Ibid., 193.
49. Ibid., 195, 194.
50. Ibid., 202. Polanyi agrees on this point as well: "Though I deny that truth is demonstrable, I assert that it is knowable" (SFS, 82).
51. Ibid., 205. Polanyi calls this anticipation of an unknown reality "intuition." He writes: "We can pursue scientific discovery without knowing what we are looking for, because the gradient of deepening coherence tells us where to start and which way to turn, and eventually brings us to the point where we may stop and claim victory" (CI, 116).
52. Ibid., 222.

53. Voegelin, *The New Science of Politics*, 169, 173; *Order and History,* IV, 28.
54. *Science, Politics and Gnosticism*, 11; *Order and History*, I, 4.
55. Voegelin, "The Beginning and Beyond."205.
56. Voegelin employs this Polanyian phrase in *The New Science of Politics*, 172.
57. Voegelin, *Order and History*, IV, 28.
58. Voegelin, *Order and History*, I, 1.
59. Voegelin, *Order and History*, IV, 28.
60. Voegelin, *The New Science of Politics*, 8, 21. Cf. PK, 3.
61. Voegelin, *The New Science of Politics*, 11–12.
62. Polanyi, who died in 1976, did not have the opportunity to comment on MacIntyre's later work. He did, however, write a brief review of MacIntyre's first book, *Marxism: An Interpretation*. It is a generally favorable review, although Polanyi chides the youthful MacIntyre for lacking "political maturity." See Michael Polanyi, "Marx and Saint Paul," *The Manchester Guardian*, March 17, 1953, 4. The two met in 1969, when Polanyi delivered a series of lectures at the University of Texas at Austin. During that time, Polanyi participated in a group discussing "Scientific Knowledge and Discovery." Marjorie Grene, Charles Taylor, Alasdair MacIntyre, and others took part (Scott and Moleski, *Michael Polanyi*, 272). It is of interest to note that both Polanyi and MacIntyre acknowledge a debt to Marjorie Grene. See the acknowledgments to PK, ix, and the preface to *After Virtue*, x, 2nd ed. (Notre Dame, IN: University of Notre Dame Press, 1988).
63. See Martha Nussbaum, "Recoiling from Reason," *New York Review*, Dec. 7 (1989), 36–41.
64. As early as 1978, Marjorie Grene pointed out the important similarities between Polanyi and MacIntrye. See "Response to Alasdair MacIntyre," *Morals, Science and Sociality*, ed. H. Tristram Engelhardt Jr. and Daniel Callahan (Hastings-on-Hudson, NY: Hastings Center, 1978), 40–47.
65. MacIntyre regularly informs his readers of his shifting beliefs, at various times describing himself as an "Augustinian Christian" (*Whose Justice, Which Rationality?* Notre Dame, IN: University of Notre Dame Press, 1988, 10); a "Thomistic Aristotelian" (*Dependent Rational Animals*, Chicago: Open Court, 1999, xi); a "Thomistic Aristotelian" and a "Catholic" ("How Can We Learn What *Veritatis Splendor* Has to Teach?" *Thomist* 58, 1994, 172); and simply as "a Thomist" in *Common Truths: New Perspectives on Natural Law*, ed. Edward B. McLean (Wilmington, DE: ISI Books, 2000), 93–94.
66. Alasdair MacIntyre, *First Principles, Final Ends and Contemporary Philo-*

sophical Issues (Milwaukee, WI: Marquette University Press, 1990), 42–43.

67. Alasdair MacIntyre, "Epistemological Crises, Dramatic Narrative and the Philosophy of Science," *Monist* 60 (1977), 465.

68. Ibid., 461.

69. Alasdair MacIntyre, "Objectivity in Morality," *Morals, Science and Sociality*, 27.

70. It should be noted at this point that MacIntyre only mentions Polanyi once in his so-called Virtue Trilogy and then only in passing: MacIntyre, *Three Rival Versions of Moral Enquiry*, 24.

71. MacIntyre, *After Virtue*, 221–22.

72. MacIntyre, *Whose Justice? Which Rationality?* 8, 353. Presumably this implies that Polanyi, too, theorized shoddily and was an agent of positive harm.

73. Ibid., 353.

74. The term postmodern is not one that Polanyi uses, but he identifies many of the features of late modernity that have come to be called postmodern.

75. This reaction was, in MacIntyre's view, inevitable. Given the premises of the Enlightenment project, that project had to fail. See chapter 5 of *After Virtue*, "Why the Enlightenment Project of Justifying Morality Had to Fail."

76. MacIntyre, *Three Rival Versions of Moral Enquiry*, 59.

77. Ibid., 59–60.

78. Ibid., 67.

79. Cf. Polanyi, TD, 92; PK, 324.

INDEX

a

adsorption, theory of, 1, 4–5, 6–7
Anglican Book of Common
 Prayer, 117
Anselm, Saint, 150–51
anti-Semitism, 11, 12–13, 121
Aquinas, Thomas, 155
Aristotle, 36, 53, 108, 155
Augustine, Saint, 58, 67, 150
 conversion and, 93, 95
 tacit knowledge, theory of
  and, 60–63
authority
 apprenticeship and, 63–64
 empiricism and, 36, 37
 freedom and, 50–52
 knowledge and, 53, 63–65
 rationalism and, 36
 religion and, 54
 science and, xii, 8, 15, 69
 skepticism and, 37

b

Bacon, Francis, 53, 63, 157
belief
 community and, 68–70
 freedom and, 59
 knowledge and, 62–63, 68–
  69, 91, 96
 language and, 69
 reason and, 62–63, 86
 See also faith
Bergson, Henri, 135
Berlin, Isaiah, 17
Berlin, University of, 12
Bernal, J. D., 41, 42
"Beyond Nihilism" (Polanyi),
 139–40
biology, 132–33
Bredig, Georg, 4
British Association for the
 Advancement of Sciences, 14
Buchböck, Gustav, 4–5

Planck, Max, 12
planned economics
  complexity and, 22–23
  human finitude and, 22
  market system vs., 21–22
  polycentric vs., 22–25, 34
  in Soviet Union, 23–25, 32–33
Plato (Meno's Paradox), 79
Poincaré, Henri, 80
Polanyi, George, 11
Polanyi, John, 11
Polanyi, Karl
  economics and, 29–35
  Galileo Circle and, 3, 29
Polanyi, Michael
  adsorption, theory of and, 1,
    4–5, 6–7
  Catholicism of, 10–11, 118
  Christianity and, 10–11, 117–22
  conservative movement and,
    138–40
  economics and, 21–28, 32–5
  education of, 1, 2–6
  Galileo Circle and, 3
  legacy of, 19–20, 162–69
  MacIntyre, Alasdair and,
    154–62
  marriage of, 11
  meaning and, 105–13
  morality and, 114–17
  Oakeshott, Michael and,
    141–44
  politics and, 8–10, 52–58
  religion and, 117–22, 122–27
  science and, 35–52
  scientific method and, 6–7,
    38

  tacit knowledge, theory of
    and, 59–103
  Voegelin, Eric and, 144–54
  x-ray fiber analysis and, 12
politics, 8–10, 52–58
  economics and, 33–35
  freedom and, xiii, 165–66
  moral inversion and, 56–57,
    140
  tradition and, 66
Pollacsek, Mihaly, 2–3
Polya, George, 16, 19
polycentricity, centralized
  economics vs., 22–25
positivism, 19, 36–37, 147
Possessed, The (Dostoyevsky), 57
Prosch, Harry, 18–19, 52, 119
Proslogion (Anselm), 151
Protestantism, 121–22
pseudo-substitution, 57
pure science
  applied vs., 13–14, 40, 42–44
  goal of, 14
  intrinsic good of, 42
  knowledge and, 43

r

rationalism
  authority and, 36
  Enlightenment, 20, 141, 159–
    60
  faith and reason and, 128
  Greek, 60–61, 62
  religion and, 127
  tradition and, 36
"Rationalism in Politics"
  (Oakeshott), 142

faith and reason and, 128–31
focal vs. subsidiary awareness
    and, 70–79, 128
indwelling and, 77
knower, role of and, 77–79,
    101–2, 168–69
objective detachment and,
    76, 79
objectivism of and, 95–97
realism and, 79–85
religion and, 118–19
subjective-objective divide
    and, 90–99
subjectivism and, 142
tacit knowing, four aspects of
    and, 74–76
tradition and, 64–68
See also knowing; knowledge
Teilhard de Chardin, Pierre, 135
Terry Lectures, Yale University, 18
Tillich, Paul, 117, 121, 131–32
Tolstoy, Leo, 10
Torrance, Thomas, 119, 120, 121–
    22
totalitarianism, 137
    freedom and, 47, 50
    philosophical roots of, 52–53
    Polanyi, Michael and, xi, 33
    transcendent values and, 46
"To the Peacemakers: Views on
    the Prerequisites of War and
    Peace in Europe" (Polanyi),
    8–9
tradition, 63–8
    community and, 68
    dynamism of, 67–8
    freedom and, 67

knowledge and, 53, 61, 64–68
MacIntyre, Alasdair and,
    159–60
modern philosophy and, 61
orthodoxy and, 67, 68
politics and, 66
rationalism and, 36
science and, xii, 15
skepticism and, 37
"Tradition and the Individual
    Talent" (Eliot), 51
transcendent values
    commitment to, xii, 15–16
    community and, 50
    science and, xii, 15–16, 46
    society and, 46
    totalitarianism and, 46
Turgenev, Ivan, 56

U

U.S.S.R..
    See Soviet Union
utilitarianism
    freedom and, 47
    morality and, 164

V

values
    See transcendent values
Van Cott, Norman, 27–28
Voegelin, Eric, 144–54

W

Watson, J. D., 107
Weathermen, 140
Weaver, Richard, 139
Wigner, E. P., 17

ABOUT THE AUTHOR

Mark T. Mitchell is Assistant Professor of Government at Patrick Henry College in Purcellville, Virginia.